Strong Faith

5 Questions and Answers Every Christian Should Know

General Editor and Contributor
T. J. Gentry

Additional Contributors
Deanna Huff
Tony Williams
Brian Chilton
Michelle Johnson

IHP Practica

IHP Practica
An Imprint of Illative House Press, LLC
500 E. Elm St.
West Frankfort, IL 62896

IllativeHousePress.com

Hardcover ISBN: 979-8-9915912-3-2
Paperback ISBN: 979-8-9915912-1-8
E-book ISBN: 979-8-9915912-2-5

Cover design by Casey Sernaque for Illative House Press. Slight modifications were made by IHP to the original design for layout and marketing purposes.

ILLATIVE
HOUSE

PRESS

Contents

Read Me First! (aka Introduction)

T. J. Gentry

The year was 1983, it was early September, and I was a freshman at Carterville High School. As I made my way through the hallways and rushed to my Physical Education class, I was excited. I was a football player (my one and only year playing, by the way), and my coach was also the PE teacher. I thought we (the football players) might get some kind of special treatment because our teacher was, after all, our coach. Maybe we'd sit around and talk about last night's practice or our upcoming game. I didn't know what to expect, but I did expect something special.

I quickly changed into my gym clothes and gathered with my classmates to wait. Out came my coach. He took attendance. Made a few announcements. Then he turned to the football players in the class. He gathered us off to the side while the rest of the class began their assigned activity. Seeing this, I said to myself, "Just as I thought. We're getting special treatment. It's good to be a football player!" That's when my coach announced that we would not do regular PE. Instead, our focus was on strength training. He pointed to the weight machines on the stage in the gym, telling us to get to it. "Wait a minute!" I thought, "We have strength training instead of regular PE?" I knew what that meant. It meant I would be sore tomorrow. It meant I had to work out, focusing on specific exercises for football. It meant PE was not going to be easy.

I grumbled under my breath, moped my way up the stairs to the stage, and started lifting. The season came and went, and I thought for sure we would have different PE after football was over. I was wrong. Football players had to do strength training all year. After all, when one season ends another begins (at least the preparation). Guess what happened that year? I lifted weights and I got stronger. Even though I fell in love with golf that spring and never played football again because the seasons were at the same time, I never forgot the lesson: Getting stronger takes effort.

That's why this book is so important. Even though we won't lift weights instead of playing dodgeball or kitten ball (maybe that's a new one to you…it has nothing to do with cats), we will learn some important things about the Christian faith. Things that are essential. Things that, if you know them, will help your faith grow strong. What we're after in this book is a strong faith, one that knows what is true, why it's true, and how to answer those who challenge its truth.

Think of the authors of the chapters as your coaches. They (we) are here to help you grow stronger in your walk with God and your witness to others. Each of us has been where you are. We all asked questions. Still do. We all found answers. You'll do the same if you try, and we hope you will. Your faith is not a wish, not a myth, and not an excuse. Your faith is built on a solid foundation of truth, and you can have strong faith.

Each of the chapters answers a specific question, and those questions are not randomly selected. Just like different exercises in the weight room, each question focuses on one area where strength is needed. But the questions are also related. They build on each other. We'll start by asking, "What is truth?" That's the foundation for the foundation. From there, we'll ask, "Does God exist?" We'll see that He does. Then we'll consider, "Is the Bible reliable?" This is the middle and central question for a reason. If the Bible is reliable (and you'll learn that it certainly is), then we can know God exists and what it means to say something is true. Our fourth question digs into the message of the Bible—it's most important message—asking, "Did Jesus rise form the dead?" You'll learn that the resurrection of Jesus has loads of proof, offers living power to our walk with God, and is the linchpin in our witness to others. All of this leads to our final question, "Is Christianity the only way?" That question is the capstone in our strength training, the exercise that demonstrates our hard work has paid off. We'll see that Jesus is the only way, and that the way is open to everyone. It just takes someone with strong faith to know and share that message. Are you ready to be that someone? Are you ready for strong faith? It's time. Let the workout begin.

PS: You'll notice that each chapter follows a similar format. The question is posed, a Scripture and important quote are offered, and an overview of the chapter is presented (that's the "What We'll Learn" heading). Then, each chapter presents three sections. Section One: Answering the Question; Section Two: Addressing Objections; and Section Three: Applying the Answer in Our Walk and in Our Witness. The chapters conclude with the Chapter Review, Learning Check, Discussion Questions, and Resources for Further Study. We used this structure for the chapters so you would have a handy way to go back to key sections, dig deeper with questions and helpful resources, and make the book easy to use for group study. Now, let's hit the weights!

Q1: What Is Truth?

T. J. Gentry

> "If you abide in My word,
> you are My disciples indeed.
> And you shall know the truth,
> and the truth shall make you free."
> John 8:31-32, NKJV[1]
>
> "You never know how much you really believe anything
> until its truth or falsehood becomes a matter
> of life and death to you."
> C. S. Lewis[2]

Why Start Here?

I've bought a lot of "assembly required" office furniture over the years. Desks, bookshelves, filing cabinets, and a whole bunch of chairs have come in and out of my various offices. Years ago, I'd open the box and start to assemble whatever the furniture item was. I might look at the picture on the box as a guide, but I rarely read the instructions. I lacked patience and had too much confidence, so I broke several bookshelves and a few desks before I learned an important lesson. Learn to read the instructions. This chapter is like the instruction manual. It's the first chapter for a good reason. Sure, you could jump ahead to the other chapters, but to get the most out of them I hope you'll trust me when I encourage you to start here. While we won't talk about assembling desks or chairs in this chapter, we will discuss an important word that the other chapters rely on. That word is truth.

If you want to know why those other chapters say what they do, you need to understand something about truth. Does God exist? Yes. Is the Bible reliable? Yes. Did Jesus rise from the dead? Yes. Is Christianity the only way? Yes. As you'll find out, the chapters following this one will give you evidence, and a lot of it, as to why it is true that Yes is the answer to those four questions. But before we talk about the truths presented in the other chapters, we need to talk about what truth is. Before we talk about things to think about that will help you have a strong faith, we need to talk about how to think about things. That's why we need to start here. So, let's get started!

What We'll Learn

Here's a summary of what we'll learn in this chapter. When I was in the Army, this section of a presentations was called "Here's what I'm gonna tell you." Or, if you like to think of a chapter as a road trip, you could refer to this section as: "Here where we're headed." Whichever you prefer, here are our learning objectives:

- Section One: Answering the Question

  We start by asking: What is truth? We'll learn that truth is what corresponds to reality, that truth certainly exists, that we can know truth, and that truth is an essential part in deciding what we believe.

- Section Two: Addressing an Objection

  While there are several objections that are raised against the idea of truth, one of the most common is: You have your truth, but I have mine. We'll look closely at this objection and see that it doesn't hold up too well in the light of common sense.

- Section Three: Applying the Answer

  Knowing how to answer our question and address a common objection is a good starting point, but applying the answer in our walk with the Lord and our witness is also important. So, our final section focuses on practical application.

Section One
Answering the Question

Sometimes the best way to answer a question is by asking another question. If my daughter asks, "Dad, do you want to try one of the cookies I baked?", then I'm likely to answer her question with a question: "What kind of cookies are they?" It would be rare that I refuse a cookie from my daughter, but I still want to know what kind they are! (For the record, my daughter is a great baker, and I've never met a cookie I didn't like.) The point is questions can help us answer questions. So, in this first section we approach our main question (What is truth?) by asking three other questions. Before we talk about each one, I'll tell you what they are:

- Does truth exist?
- How can we know the truth?
- How does truth relate to faith?

Does Truth Exist?

This is a tricky question. Unless we refuse to answer it, any answer we give is a way of saying, "Yes. Truth exists." How so? Well, if we answer that we don't know if truth exists, we are making a claim that it is true that we don't know if truth exists. That means we know at least one thing is true—that we aren't sure if truth exists. If we say truth doesn't exist, we come to the same place—we know that at least one truth exists, the truth that truth does not exist. Of course, if we answer that we think truth exists then we need to explain what we mean by truth. This gets us into the realm of what is real, I mean *really* real. If you're tempted to check-out at this point, thinking this is getting weird and too philosophical (I know a lot of people don't like philosophy, at least what they think it is) then I ask you to hang on and see if we can make sense of this together. I think we can!

What is *real*? A quick dictionary search comes up with the following definition: "actually existing as a thing or occurring in fact; not imagined or supposed."[3] This definition is an adjective, which our English teachers taught us is a word that describes a noun or pronoun. (Thank you, English teachers!) But wait, what's the word being described when we say something is real? This gets us to another definition, the word *reality*. What is reality? If we go to the dictionary one more time, we learn that reality (a noun) is "the world or state of things as they actually exist."[4] What does this have to do with truth? Simply stated, truth is what is real. Truth is what exists as reality. Or, to put it in more official philosophical language, truth is what corresponds to reality.

Do you think anything is real? Is the book you're holding in your hand or viewing on your screen real? Do the words on this page exist? Are the questions I just asked real questions? Do they correspond with (represent) reality? I think we know the answers to what I'm asking. We know that there are some things that really exist. Even if we're not sure how to explain how we know that some things exist, we know the difference between fiction and non-fiction. For example, I doubt any of us think the wizard Gandolf from *The Lord of the Rings* is a real person.

We might love his character, appreciate J. R. R. Tolkien for imagining him and his story, and even dress up like him for fun, but we know Gandolf is not real. Nobody doubts that Tolkien was a real person, though. We can say with confidence that it is true that Tolkien was born January 3, 1892, in Bloemfontein, South Africa, and died September 2, 1973, in Bournemouth, England. We can be certain he was a professor at the Universities of Leeds and Oxford, and that he was a friend of C. S. Lewis.[5] Tolkien is real. Gandolf is not. Knowing the difference in these two statements points us in the direction of how we can know if something is true or not true. And this brings us to our next question, one that we need to ask if we want to know what is real. Here it is: How can we know the truth?

How Can We Know the Truth?

If we want to determine if something is true, we start by looking at the evidence. This is an important point for us to remember in our search for truth. If something is true, there will be evidence. Now, having evidence doesn't make something true, but if something is true, there will be evidence. In other words, evidence is part (a big part!) of knowing what is true. For example, I could tell you there is a shoeprint in the dirt in my backyard. I could also tell you that it was made by the President of the United States. You might think this sounds suspicious, but I'm convinced it was the President. I present the following as evidence: the shoeprint was made by a shoe that matches the shoes worn by the President; the shoe size is the same as the President's; and the depth of the shoeprint is consistent with someone of the President's height and weight. Do I have evidence? Yes. Is the evidence enough to prove the

President was walking around in my backyard? Not exactly. I would have to have additional evidence to show that it is true that the President was in my backyard.

I'm pretty stubborn, so when you continue to doubt my story, I offer to show you my security video from the timeframe when the shoeprint was made. Here's the thing, though, I haven't looked at the video yet. But I'm confident based on the evidence I have, so we pull up the video on my phone. Sure enough, there's someone in my backyard. Does that prove my claim? Not yet. What can we do? We enlarge the video shot to see that the person wearing those shoes was not the President. It was my son! Boy, I'm embarrassed. I claimed something was true based on some evidence, but when more evidence was examined, my claim proved false. While my son may have great taste in shoes, he's not the President. So, how did we show that my initial claim is false and that what is true—what corresponds to reality—is something else? We examined more evidence, and that's what we always must do to know what's true. Remember, truth is what corresponds to reality, and if something's real there will be evidence.

This brings us to another question, though. How do we examine evidence? Do we need to go to an evidence examination school? Become a detective? Well, if we want to solve crimes, we probably need that type of training. But each of us already have what we need to know if truth claims are *actually* true—we have a mind and a heart. You may be thinking: "Wait a minute. Did you say mind *and* heart? I thought truth was all about the mind and logic and reason." You're right to think the pursuit of truth involves the mind and logic and reason. But reason involves more than the mind; it also involves the heart. We evaluate evidence with our minds *and* our hearts. Our thoughts and our feelings are different but they're not completely separate. This may be a new idea for you, but it's called passional or whole-person reason. Our mind informs our heart, and our heart informs our mind. It may be that one is primary (usually the mind), but the other is always involved when it comes to what we choose to believe is true. In other words, the reasons for believing something is true come from our examination of evidence with our minds and our hearts.

We need a bit of caution here, though, as we can become unbalanced between mind and heart. Some people refuse to let their emotions have any say in what they believe is true, while others barely engage their minds and are driven by emotion. Both approaches create problems, and balance is the goal. It may help you to think (and feel!) this way about what I'm saying: If something is true there will be evidence that is both logical and objective (known by the mind) *and* emotional and subjective (known by the heart). Knowing what is true is not *either* mind or heart but *both* mind and heart. We discern truth with our whole person, mind and heart.

Based on what we've learned, we need to ask one more question: How does truth relate to faith? This question is important—very important—for what is presented in the remaining chapters of this book. Here's why: In the remaining chapters we're not simply asking if it's true that Gandolf is real or whether the President was in my backyard. We're talking about essential truth claims of the Christian faith:

- Does God exist?
- Is the Bible reliable?

- Did Jesus rise from the dead?
- Is Christianity the only way?

If the evidence reveals that the true answer to any of these questions is No, then we have a problem. If God doesn't exist, then the Bible's claims that He does are false, and Scripture is unreliable. If Scripture is unreliable, then we have reason to doubt its claims that Jesus rose from the dead (that is an amazing claim, after all) and that Christianity is the only way to salvation. There's a lot at stake when it comes to the questions of what's true, how we know what's true, and how truth relates to faith. Ultimately, what we're considering is if we can know that Christianity is true and should we have faith in its message.

How Does Truth Relate to Faith?

For starters, it's important to know that we decide what we will believe. Believing and unbelieving are choices. Every person can choose to believe or choose not to believe. And these choices are not limited to matters of religion. I can choose to believe Gandolf is real, and that the President was in my backyard. My choices wouldn't be based on reality. My choices would be despite the evidence, but they would still be my choices and my beliefs. Likewise, I can choose to believe Tolkien is real, and that my son was in my backyard. Those choices would be based on the evidence, and my beliefs would be true because they correspond to reality. (Please keep these points in mind as we talk about truth and faith.)

Where does this leave us regarding the relationship between truth and faith? To answer this, let's define faith in the language the Bible uses in Hebrews 11:1, "Faith is the reality of what is hoped for, the proof of what is not seen" (CSB). Notice the words *reality* and *proof*? By using these words to define faith, we can make a few important statements about what Christians *should* mean when they talk about faith. First, faith isn't blind. It looks at what's real and what has proof. Second, faith isn't contrary to evidence. It's based on evidence. Now let's make a few other important points about faith. First, reality and proof are not the same things as faith. Second, evidence is not the same thing as faith. Reality, proof, and evidence can lead to faith, but they're not the same as faith.

Maybe at this point you're thinking, "Okay, okay. Why are you making these points?" Here's why. Faith is a step beyond reality, proof, and evidence. It's not contrary to those things, but it is a decision the mind and heart make to trust what reality, proof, and evidence point to. In this case, reality, proof, and evidence point to God. Remember, Christians are not saved by reality, proof, and evidence. Christians are saved by faith (Eph. 2:8-9), but that faith is based on the reality, proof, and evidence of what God has revealed in the world, in Scripture, and in Jesus. Going back to Hebrews 11:1, that's why faith is tied to "what is hoped for" and "what is not seen."

As the other chapters in this book will show, there's more than enough real evidence (truth) that speaks to the heart and mind to support a decision to believe in Christianity's message (the Bible) and Messenger (Jesus). It's also possible to choose not to believe in Christianity, but it isn't due to a lack of evidence. Unbelief is a choice to interpret the evidence another way. Same evidence, different choice. And there are those who choose not to believe. Why is that? Well, it's not because they can't believe; it's because they won't believe. To clarify this a bit, let's consider what God desires. He is "not wanting any to perish but all to come to repentance" (2 Pet. 3:9 CSB). Why is God so concerned? "God is love" (1 John 4:8 CSB), and He "so loved the world that He gave His only begotten Son, that whoever believes in Him should not perish but have eternal life" (John 3:16 NKJV). So, God's love motivated Him to give Jesus to save anyone who believes. But can all believe? Yes. "God wants everyone to be saved and to come to the knowledge of the truth" (1 Tim. 2:4 CSB), which means that even though sin affects everyone and everything (Eph. 2:1-7), and no one could ever choose to believe in God without His grace (Eph. 2:8-9), God's choice to love all people means He gives all of us the power to choose to believe or not to believe. No one can save themselves, but everyone can believe and be saved. Everyone includes you. Everyone includes me. Everyone means everyone.

With this in mind, let's address an objection to what we learned about truth being what corresponds to reality. While this isn't the only objection you'll hear, it's one that comes up a lot. Here it is: You have your truth, but I have mine.

Section Two
Addressing an Objection

We all have opinions. In my opinion, raisin pie is the best kind of pie. Sure, I like other pies, but raisin pie is the best! At least that's my opinion. You're probably chuckling right now, either wondering what raisin pie is, or asking why anyone would think raisin pie is the best. There are only a few of us who love raisin pie, after all. Still, it's okay to have an opinion about pie and many other things. But what is an opinion? It's a personal view or attitude.[6] An opinion is a real thing to the person who has it, but is an opinion the same thing as truth? Not necessarily. It's true that my favorite pie is raisin pie, but it's not true that raisin pie is everyone's favorite or even the best pie ever made. That's the thing about opinions, they are all subject to the thoughts and feelings of those who have them. (I feel pretty strongly about raisin pie!)

Opinions are fine as far as they go and even make life interesting, but when opinions take the place of truth a problem arises. For example, if you warn me that stepping in front of a car moving at 100 miles per hour will cause great bodily harm and likely death, would that be a matter of opinion or is your warning a matter of truth? What if I respond to your warning with, "Well, that's your truth but not mine. I don't think it's true, so it doesn't apply to me."? I hope you will tell me that truth isn't a matter of mere opinion, and it's not the case that being harmed by stepping in front of a fast-moving car is only true for you but not me. That you will urge me not to confuse opinion with truth. And remind me that truth is what corresponds to reality, and it's a reality that anyone who steps in front of a fast-moving car is going to be hurt and probably die. (Thanks for your concern, by the way. I'll stay out of the road!)

How does the difference we've identified between truth and opinion relate to our main question in this chapter: What is truth? Although there are several areas we could talk about, let's focus on just one. Let's focus on morality. When it comes to what is right and what is wrong (what is moral and immoral), it's true that there are many opinions. Some are of the opinion that right and wrong are whatever we decide. If we decide it's wrong to tell lies to make ourselves look better, then we shouldn't tell lies. But if we decide it's perfectly fine to tell lies to build ourselves up in the eyes of others, then we should tell lies. In this example, the person who chooses to lie might say to the person who thinks lying is wrong, "That's true for you, but not true for me. Right and wrong are nothing more than personal preferences." However, if you insist on your view that lying is wrong, you'll soon learn that the person who disagrees with you actually does have a definite view on what's right and what's wrong. And they believe that others should agree with them.

How do we know this? Because as soon as the defender of lying says to you, "You can't tell me what's right and wrong. It's wrong of you to do that. You should just let me do what I want!", they reveal that they really don't believe that truth is up to each person to decide. What they do believe is that everyone should have their view on truth and those who don't are wrong. If they think lying about others to better their situation is okay, they usually mean that it's okay for them to do it. But if you ask them if it's okay for you to lie about them to make yourself look better, what do you think they will say? They're going to protest, saying you shouldn't do that to them. You'll soon learn that they really don't believe that right and wrong are only matters of opinion.

We could apply this same type of scenario to any number of moral concerns, and we'll come to the same conclusion. Recall that what's true is what corresponds to reality, and what's real isn't simply a matter of opinion. But this doesn't only apply to morality, to right and wrong. As the other chapters in this book will show, it's not merely a matter of opinion whether God exists, the Bible is reliable, Jesus rose from the dead, or Christianity is the only way. You'll see that the evidence is overwhelming and there are good reasons for the mind and heart to choose to believe. You'll see that strong faith is a choice, a choice based on the truth of what corresponds to reality. It may be that some choose unbelief, and that's their opinion. But that opinion doesn't mean that the truth of the evidence for Christianity is simply a matter of opinion. It's never really the case that you have your truth, and I have my truth. What's real is that truth is truth, and each person decides what to do with the truth. Deciding to reject it doesn't make it less true, nor does deciding to accept it make it more true. Our opinions matter, but the truth is unchanging. And our opinions don't change what's true. Reality is reality.

Before we move on, take a moment to congratulate yourself. Take a bow! You've come a long way in considering some pretty difficult stuff! Truth, reality, passional reason, biblical faith, and answering an objection aren't easy topics. Well done! Now we're ready to shift gears. In the next section we'll discover ways to apply what we've learned. First, we'll talk about applying what we've learned in our walk with God. After all, truth helps us grow as Christians. Second, we'll explore ways to apply what we know about truth in our witness with others. All around us there are people who don't yet know the truth and don't yet believe in Jesus. We can help them. Let's get to it!

Section Three
Applying the Answer in Our Walk and in Our Witness

Every Christian is commanded by God to grow deeper and reach wider. Jesus made this clear in giving what we call The Great Commission: "Go therefore and make disciples of all the nations, baptizing them in the name of the Father and of the Son and of the Holy Spirit, teaching them to observe all things that I have commanded you" (Matt. 28:19-20 NKJV). Growing deeper has to do with our walk with God. That's the part where Jesus commands teaching and observing, and it's by teaching and observing God's truth that we grow deeper as disciples of God and His truth. Reaching wider has to do with our witness to others. That's the part where Jesus commands us to go and make disciples, and it's by going and making that we reach wider as declarers of God's truth. It takes practice to grow deeper and reach wider, and the best practice is practical. Here, then, are a few practical ways to apply what we've learned about truth.

How Does This Answer Apply to My Walk with God?

Jesus said two really important things about truth. Both of them are in John 17:17. Here's what He said: "Sanctify them by Your truth. Your word is truth" (NKJV). Notice that the first sentence is a request, and the second is a statement. What's the request? That the Father will sanctify (set apart and make holy) the disciples by His truth. What's the statement? Jesus states that God's word is truth. But why did Jesus use the word truth two times, and what does He mean?

Let's start with a definition based on the word Jesus used (we'll see it's the same definition we already know about truth). Truth in John 17:17 comes from the Greek word *aletheia* (al-ay-thi-a), which means what is factual and real.[7] Sound familiar? It should. We've already talked about the definition of truth as what is real, what corresponds to reality (if you need a refresher, go to Section One). Jesus didn't make up this word. It was common in His day, and why is that? Because even 2,000 years ago people understood that truth exists, and that truth is what corresponds to reality. So, if you wonder if Jesus thought truth exists and is what corresponds to reality, now you know. But He's teaching us more in John 17:17 than just that truth exists. He's talking about the standard of truth ("Your word") and the power of truth ("Sanctify them"). As we dig deeper into what Jesus means by standard and power, we'll find two ways what we know about truth can help us grow in our walk with God.

1. Learn That God's Word Is the Standard of Truth.

When it comes to God's word (the Bible) as the standard of truth this means that even though the Bible doesn't contain all truth (you won't find 2+2=4 in there), anything that is true (real) is consistent with and does not contradict what God says. Why? Because truth ultimately comes from God. He is truth and truth exists because God exists (more about that in the next chapter). Another was to say this is that all truth is God's truth. Sometimes we'll find truth surrounded by lies. Does that make the truth untrue? No. What's true is true, regardless of where we find it. Our job is to recognize all truth wherever we find it and claim it as God's, since it's already His. When we do this, we grow in our walk with God. We become more confident in what truth is, where it comes from, and we learn what error looks like because we're so familiar with truth. But it all starts with God's word. His word is our first and final standard of truth. Grow in your walk with God by learning that all truth is God's truth, especially His word.

2. Let God's Truth Speak to Our Mind and Heart.

Remember when we learned about passional or whole-person reason? The mind *and* the heart? That's how we explained what it means to determine what is real (what is true) and then choose to believe (have faith) based on evidence and proof of what is true. Well, when we think about the way we believe with our mind and our heart we can understand why Jesus prayed, "Sanctify them by Your truth" (John 17:17 NKJV). All truth is important, but "the word of God is living and powerful...a discerner of the thoughts and intents of the heart" (Heb. 4:12 NKJV). Did you catch that? God's word—the standard of truth—is alive. It's powerful. It reveals our thoughts and intentions. Wow! Think about that for a moment and let it sink in. As we choose to make God's word our standard of truth, spending time reading and studying it, it reveals our thoughts and intentions. Why would God want it to do that? He knows that our thoughts and intentions can and should transform so that we better know Him (and He is truth). He knows that when we come to the Bible with a desire to learn and a decision to grow in faith, we will "be transformed by the renewing of [our] mind" (Rom. 12:2a NKJV). Why does this matter? As our mind (and heart) are renewed by God's word, we can "discern what is the good, pleasing, and perfect will of God" (Rom 12:2b CSB). Is God's will for us to live in error or walk in truth? He wants us to walk in truth—to know it, trust it, explain it, defend it— so that we can be made free by it. Never forget that Jesus said, "If you abide (live) in My word, you are My disciples indeed. And you shall know the truth, and the truth shall make you free" (John 8:31-32 NKJV). We grow in our walk with God as we let His word speak to our mind and heart. This is why getting to know the Bible is so important.

How Does This Answer Apply to My Witness to Others?

Jesus wants us to grow deeper *and* reach wider. Since we just talked about growing deeper, let's talk about reaching wider and how our knowledge of truth can help. Reaching wider has to do with witnessing, with talking to others about why we believe the Christian message is true. Some people we know are skeptical of anything to do with our faith, especially when we talk about truth. Others are curious, they're seeking to know more but aren't quite ready to believe. God cares about both, the skeptic and the seeker. He loves them, and He chooses to use us to show His love to them. We do that in different ways, depending on the person and circumstance. However, what we know about truth—that truth is what corresponds to reality—can help us help them. In addition to learning the questions and answers this book gives (and that will help a lot with your walk and your witness), here are two ways the specific focus of this chapter applies to our witness.

1. Talk to the Skeptics and the Seekers in Your Life.

Make sure to listen more than you talk, and ask questions! Here are a few questions that might help start a conversation:

- Do you think anything is true?
- How would you know if something was true?
- Is truth the same thing as faith?

Asking these questions can be a little scarry (or a lot!), especially if you think you should be able to explain everything about truth. Relax, that's not your goal. Your goal is to have a conversation, learn what your skeptic and seeker friends think, and then offer the answers and insights you've learned in this chapter. What you need is courage and faith. Be courageous, start a conversation, and have faith that God is with you. He is.

2. Pray for the Skeptics and Seekers in Your Life.

Pray for them by name. Pray for them daily. Ask God to help you better grasp what truth is, why it matters, and for the opportunity to talk to your skeptic and seeker friends. As you pray for them, remind yourself that they are more than their skepticism or seeking. They are image bearers of God. They have dignity and worth, and they decide what they will believe. You can't force faith, but you can make it attractive by thinking and speaking clearly about truth. Ask God to let you see beyond their questions to the questioner. To let you see past their objections to the objector. To help you love them by speaking up for truth.

Chapter Review

We've come to the end of our journey in this chapter. We've covered a lot of ground and, hopefully, learned the truth about truth along the way. Before we move on to the next chapter and next question in our quest for strong faith, let's review. (This is also a great section in the chapter to turn to again and again for a quick refresher on the main points we covered!)

In the first section, we focused on answering the chapter question: What is truth? We sought our answer by asking three additional questions: Does truth exist? How can we know the truth? How does truth relate to faith? Here's what we found:

- Does truth exist?
  - Yes. Truth is what is real, what corresponds to reality.
- How can we know the truth?
  - We can know the truth by reasoning with our whole person, mind and heart. This is called passional reason.
- How does truth relate to faith?
  - Faith is a decision to trust based on what the mind and heart reasonably conclude is true based on the evidence. God loves

everyone and His grace enables everyone to know the truth and to believe.

In the second section, we addressed a common objection to our definition that truth is what corresponds to reality: You have your truth, but I have mine. In thinking through this objection, we learned that:

- There is a difference between opinion and truth.
- We all have opinions, but truth is not merely an opinion.
- Even someone who claims that truth is whatever we want it to be doesn't really believe that or live consistently with that claim.

In the third section, we talked about how knowing that truth is what corresponds to reality applies to our walk with God and our witness with others. This is important because God expects us to grow deeper (in our walk with Him) and reach wider (in our witness to others). The groundwork for building on how truth applies to our walk with God came from John 17:17, where Jesus made a prayer and a statement concerning truth: "Sanctify them by Your truth. Your word is truth" (NKJV). In these words, Jesus reveals God's word as the standard and the power of truth. With this in mind, we considered two ways truth applies in our walk:

1. We grow as we learn that God's word is the standard of truth.
2. We grow as we let God's truth speak to our mind and heart.

Then, we discussed the importance of our witness to truth. God places skeptics and seekers in our lives, and His love for them is expressed through us as we share what truth is and why it matters. To help with our witness, we identified two ways:

1. We grow in our witness as we have conversations with the skeptics and seekers in our lives, remembering to listen more than we talk and to ask good questions:

   - Do you think anything is true?

   - How would you know if something was true?

   - Is truth the same thing as faith?

2. We grow in our witness as we pray for the skeptics and seekers in our lives, remembering who they are as image bearers of God and asking God to help us love them by speaking up for truth.

Learning Check

Here are five questions to check your learning:

1. Define truth.
2. Define passional or whole-person reason.
3. Explain the relationship between reason and faith.
4. Answer the objection, "You have your truth, but I have mine."
5. Explain what Jesus taught in John 17:17.

Discussion Questions

Here are five questions to prompt a meaningful discussion:

1. What objections to the definition of truth as what corresponds to reality have you heard? How did you respond?
2. Do you agree that mind and heart are both involved in reasoning about evidence? Why or why not?
3. Why does it matter that biblical faith is not blind?
4. In addition to the ways given in the chapter, how could you apply the truth about truth in your walk with God? In your witness with others?
5. How does this chapter help you grow stronger in your faith?

Resources for Further Study

- "Is Anything Really, Truly True?" by J. Warner Wallace. Video available at https://youtu.be/Dk166EukC_4?si=FPp6jv8ovq7La2w2.

- "Defenders' Q&A" by T. J. Gentry. Audio available at https://www.sermonaudio.com/series/163069.

- "My Dear Apologist: Please, Be Patient" by T. J. Gentry. Article available at https://www.moralapologetics.com/wordpress/2020/8/31/my-dear-apologist-please-be-patient?rq=Gentry

- "All Truth Is God's Truth" by Alan Shlemon. Article available at https://www.str.org/w/all-truth-is-god-s-truth?p_l_back_url=%2Fsearch%3Fq%3Dtruth

- *Pocket Handbook of Christian Apologetics* by Peter Kreeft and Ronald Tacelli.

Q2: Does God Exist?

Deanna Huff

> **"The heavens are telling**
> **of the glory of God;**
> **and their expanse is declaring**
> **the work of His hands."**
> Psalm 19:1, NASB[8]
>
> **"The great pioneers in physics–Newton, Galileo, Kepler,**
> **Copernicus–devoutly believed themselves called to find**
> **evidences of God in the physical world."**
> Stephen Meyer[9]

What We'll Learn

Have you ever had doubts that God exists? C.S. Lewis, a twentieth-century British literary scholar who wrote the *Chronicles of Narnia*, spoke of his own doubts. He said, "I do have moods in which the whole thing looks very improbable: but when I was an atheist I had moods in which Christianity looked terribly probable. The rebellion of your moods is going to come anyway."[10] At the end of the day, no matter what worldview you practice or explore, every ideology requires faith. You will find new information or face a new trial that shakes your faith, then doubt will arise. Many people have wrestled with doubts but there is reasonable evidence from special revelation (the Bible) and general revelation (Nature) that supports the existence of God and can relinquish doubts. Many of the great pioneers of science explored the natural world, such as Galileo, Johannes Kepler, and Isaac Newton, who believed they could uncover patterns of the world because there was order in the world by an intelligent designer. Many scientists believed that the designer was the God of the Bible. In the Scriptures, Genesis proclaims, "In the beginning God created the heavens and the earth" (Gen 1:1). In this chapter, you will learn two arguments that people use to make a compelling case for God's existence. The cosmological argument and the fine-tuning argument can strengthen your faith in God and provide you with meaningful conversation tips to make a case for the existence of God. Here are our specific learning objectives:

- Define the cosmological and tuning fine-tuning arguments for the existence of God.

- Summarize a scientific discovery that supports an argument for the existence of God.

- Recall a question that promotes meaningful conversations about the existence of God.

Section One
Answering the Question

During college, I regularly participated in conversations about God's existence. Sometimes, people responded by saying that they didn't believe God exists. After some of those conversations it became clear that I needed to explore how to better respond to people questioning God's existence. I believed the Bible to be true, but I struggled to present convincing arguments for my beliefs. 1 Peter 3:15 instructs believers to "sanctify Christ as Lord in your hearts, always being ready to make a defense to everyone who asks you to give an account for the hope that is in you, yet with gentleness and reverence." As I began to seek answers, it became apparent that many scientists and philosophers were Christians who had provided thoughtful arguments for the existence of

God. Although there are several arguments for the existence of God this chapter will only focus on two: the Cosmological Argument and the Fine-Tuning Argument.

A World with a Beginning

Throughout the centuries, the origins of the universe have sparked debate over whether the universe has eternally existed or if there was a first cause. The first cause refers to an eternal being that has always existed and brought everything into being. During the twentieth century, scientific discoveries point favorably to a first cause. Albert Einstein, an agnostic theoretical physicist in 1915, developed the equation for general relativity, it was the beginning evidence pointing to an expanding universe. If the universe was expanding, then there must have been a beginning. In 1929, astronomer Edwin Hubble's telescope discovery would provide evidence of an expanding universe. Hubble's breakthrough came directly from the sky rather than a theory discussion.[11] The evidence offered clear support that the universe was expanding and had a beginning, which raised questions about a causal agent. Later, Stephen Hawking, Roger Penrose, and George Ellis would uncover "that there is a singularity in the past that constitutes, in some sense, a beginning of the universe."[12] These scientific breakthroughs reveal the universe has a beginning point.

William Lane Craig, a 21st-century philosopher and Christian apologist, encourages people to utilize the discoveries as a bridge to share with people that God is a reasonable first cause of the universe. He uses the cosmological argument to explain why the beginning of something existing needs a cause. "*Cosmology* represents the study of the universe."[13]

He notes, "The argument is so marvelously simple that it's easy to memorize and share with another person."[14] The cosmological argument follows:

1. Whatever begins to exist has a cause.
2. The universe began to exist.
3. Therefore, the universe has a cause.

Since it is supported that the discoveries in science point to a beginning, then the question arises: What kind of cause would it have to be to design the universe? Craig states, "The cosmological argument gives us powerful grounds for believing in the existence of a beginningless, uncaused, timeless, spaceless, changeless, immaterial, enormously powerful Personal Creator of the universe."[15] The God of the Bible offers such a being.

The Bible declares that God is evident to all people in Romans 1:20, which states, "For since the creation of the world His invisible attributes, His eternal power and divine nature, have been clearly seen, being understood through what has been made, so that they are without excuse." God desires for his people to look at the world and observe His magnificent creation. He is an eternal God who gave birth to the world as it says in Psalm 90:2, "You (God) gave birth to the earth and the world." There are meanings of self-existence and eternality seen in the revelation of His name to Moses in Exodus 3:14, "I AM, WHO I AM."

The natural world that reinforces the cosmological argument supports a case for the first cause. The first cause must be a being that is timeless, immaterial, powerful, and intelligent to create such a complex and marvelous universe. The Bible reveals God as this being. Let's now turn to the second argument that reinforces the belief that God does exist by looking at the Fine-Tuning Argument.

A World of Fine-Tuning

The 1873 story of *Goldilocks and the Three Bears* is a timeless classic about a young girl who held specific expectations amidst her adventures. Today, that story resonates in the scientific community with what is called the Goldilocks Zone. To get a quick summary of the story, Goldilocks was playing in the woods when she followed a wonderful smell in an unattended bear home. She sees three bowls with porridge on the table and tastes the first bowl, and says, "It is too cold," she moves to taste the second bowl and says, "It is too hot," and she tastes the third bowl and says, "It is just right." It is the theme of being "just right" that has been used within the scientific community in connection with the universe being just right for permitting life. Stephen Meyer, a geophysicist says, "Fine-tuning in physics refers to the discovery that many properties of the universe fall within extremely narrow and improbable rages that turn out to be absolutely necessary for complex forms of life, or even complex chemistry, and thus any conceivable form of life, to exist." This universe is "just right" for the existence of life."[16]

Astrophysicist, Sir Fred Hoyle, in the 20th century, started his career as a staunch atheist, yet he was a key contributor to the fine-tuning parameters. After recognizing the fine-tuning, he did not become a believer in God, but he did agree that there was some sort of intelligent design behind the universe. The life-permitting range is so narrow that there would be no life if the scales were titled to the slightest degree. The Bible speaks about people who see and hear but are unwilling to believe in God. Matthew 13:15 says, "You will keep on hearing, but will not understand; You will keep on seeing, but will not perceive; For the heart of this people has become dull." It is not for lack of evidence that people cannot see the evidence for God but because their hearts are unwilling to believe.

The fine-tuning argument is helpful in conversations with people who may reject intelligence as the cause of the universe. The Fine-Tuning Argument states:

1. The fine-tuning of the universe is due to either physical necessity, chance, or design.
2. The fine-tuning is not due to physical necessity or chance.
3. Therefore, it is due to design.

The Fine-Tuning Argument is full of different pieces of evidence, but we will limit it to three:

1. The Size of the Earth – If the Earth were slightly smaller or even slightly larger, then life would cease to exist.
2. The Distance of the Earth from the Sun – If the Earth were slightly closer to the Sun, the water would mostly evaporate, preventing the existence of life. On the other hand, if the Earth were slightly farther away from the Sun, then the water would be frozen, preventing life.
3. Jupiter and Saturn Prevent Meteorites – Jupiter and Saturn run interference for the Earth. These planets prevent Earth from being constantly hit with meteorites and asteroids. It is now known "that it's only the tremendous mass and gravity of these two monstrously large planets that protects us, because they pull most of these speeding objects away from us—either by simply

deflecting them into outer space or actually absorbing them into themselves."[17]

Section one laid out two arguments for the existence of God. We live in a world that has a beginning and a world that is fine-tuned. Both of these arguments raise the question, "What caused the universe to begin, and what intelligence made it perfect for life to exist? The timeless, immaterial, powerful, intelligent God of the Bible is the best explanation for the universe.

Section Two
Addressing Objections

Even though there is strong support that the God of the Bible is the best explanation for the first cause and fine-tuning, there will be some that will raise questions and objections. It can be good to hear both sides of the argument in an effort to make a reasonable decision. At times, objections can sound good on the surface, but we should listen to Proverbs 18:17, which states, "The first to plead his case seems right, until someone comes along and examines him." We want to be willing to listen and expose errors in objections to the arguments. Jesus provides an example of listening and responding to questions where people were amazed at His understanding. Luke writes about Jesus when he states, "Sitting in the midst of the teachers, both listening to them and asking them questions. And all who heard Him were amazed at His understanding and His answers." We, too, can follow the example of Jesus by listening to people and answering people's objections. In this section, we will examine a few questions and objections people might present when discussing the cosmological and fine-tuning arguments.

When talking about the origin and fine-tuning of the universe, many people will fall into one of two camps. One is scientific materialism, which means only the physical world exists from matter and energy and there are no supernatural things in the world. They would deny the existence of an immaterial, free-will God. The second camp holds to some sort of intelligence design for the universe, and Christians would say the best answer for that intelligence is the God of the Bible. Although there are more questions and objections then we will address, these will get us started in answering them.

As Christians engage with people attempting to make sense of the world and raise objections to the idea of God, remember the wise words from the book of Colossians 4:5-6, "Conduct yourselves with wisdom toward outsiders, making the most of the opportunity. Let your speech always be with grace, as though seasoned with salt." When you engage someone about the origins of the Earth, remember that scientists are regularly coming up with theories to explain the origins of the universe, but that does not mean that they have a better explanation. Sometimes objections will be presented as questions. Let's take a look at some questions and objections some people may present in your conversations.

If God Created the Universe, Who Created God?

The answer is that God is an uncaused being, meaning he has always existed. He is a timeless being. God has no beginning and no end. This may be challenging for people to grasp because mankind is in time. However, God transcends time. He is everlasting, Isaiah 40:28 describes God as everlasting, "Do you not know? Have you not heard?

The Everlasting God, the Lord, the Creator of the ends of the earth."
Someone asking the question, "Who made God?" is like someone
asking, "Who created the uncreated?" We should not make the mistake
that everything must have a cause, but instead remember that everything
that begins has a cause.

How Can God Make Something Out of Nothing?
It would be unwise to say that nothing caused something, but it is not
unwise to say that an all-powerful, transcendent free will, God, brought
the universe into existence from nothing. He has the free will to enact
creation. He is timeless, spaceless, and an immaterial being. The scientific
evidence points to the universe having a beginning and the cosmological
argument shows that a beginning must have a cause. Therefore, it is
plausible to say that God created the universe out of nothing.

Properties of the Fine-Tuning Argument Could've Been Different.
Someone may object to the fine-tuning argument by stating that the
properties of the universe could have possibly been different, and maybe
the universe would have evolved differently. And if unintelligible matter
had produced the universe, the overwhelming possible outcome would
have been a universe that prevented life. But if a designing mind created
the universe, then it would make sense that there is a fine-tuned, life-
permitting planet. Since there is a life-permitting universe, we would
expect exactly what we find, which is a fine-tuned, livable universe.

The Multiverse Theory Explains the Fine-Tuning of the Universe.
The popular notion of the multiverse is a conversation people are
having, but there is still no explanation of who created the multiverse.
The multiverse concept says there are many other universes but also

various mechanisms for generating new universes. Our universe is like a lucky winner that is life-permitting. Nothing that happens in one universe should have any effect on other universes. This theory of the multiverse is a popular idea in many shows like the Flash. However, it falls short due to a lack of evidence that one exists. It is a speculative theory to explain why there is fine-tuning in the universe. Even if a multiverse did exist, then we would be back to the question of "Who created the multiverse?"

The Fine-Tuning of the Universe Just Happened by Chance.

Some might argue that the fine-tuning of the universe just happened by chance, but the chance is so astronomical that it is almost impossible to fathom the idea. The best explanation for the beginning of the universe and fine-tuning is the God of the Bible, as noted in Isaiah 45:12, "It is I who made the earth, and created man upon it. I stretched out the heavens with My hands And I ordained all their host."

Section Three
Applying the Answer in Our Walk and in Our Witness

How Does This Answer Apply to My Walk with God?

When viewing the world, the voice of God speaks through His creation. Throughout Christian history, theologians have referred to nature as God's general revelation to people. Nature reveals the power and majesty of God. He created a beautiful world for his people. Some people believe observing the natural world reveals the character and nature of God, which at times inspires people to worship God. In Psalm 14:3-9, King David writes, "When I consider Your heavens, the work of Your fingers, The moon and the stars, which You have ordained; What is man that You take thought of him…" The displays of nature and man are the work of God's fingers, metaphorically speaking because God is Spirit. These arguments for the existence of God display the omnipotence (power) and omniscience (all-knowing) of God. It reflects His power to create a world perfectly for life. Understanding the arguments for the existence of God can strengthen your view of His attributes, it can strengthen your view of His love, and it can strengthen your faith as a Christian.

The existence of God arguments can strengthen your view of God's attributes. God created out of nothing. The transcendent and eternal being created an intelligible universe that people could study. They can look out into nature and recognize an omnipotent God created the world. God spoke of the constellation when he revealed his power to Job. This power Job could not comprehend or attain. Job 38:31-33 says, "Can you bind the chains of the Pleiades, Or loose the cords of Orion? Can you lead forth a constellation in its season, And guide the Bear with her satellites? Do you know the ordinances of the heavens, Or fix their rule over the earth?" God's power is above all things. God is all-powerful and able to accomplish what no other being can do.

The existence of God arguments can strengthen your view of His love. In thinking about love and science I am reminded of a story Dr. Carolyn Weber recounts in *Surprised by Oxford*. "She writes of a scientist named Dr. Sterling from Oxford who was once asked, 'What is the greatest force in the world?' Dr. Sterling replied, 'love.' There is nothing more powerful, more radical, more transformational than love. No other source or substance or force. And do not be deceived, for it is all of these things, and then some! The Great Love of the Universe, the

Love that sets everything in motion, keeps it in motion, moves through all things and yet bulldozes nothing, not even our will. If you love the Great Love first, because It loved you first, and then love yourself as you have been loved, and then love others from that love. There is no other force in the universe comparable to that."[18] It is this love that holds all things together and invites us to know Him. He loves his creation and people. In the beginning, He created a perfect world for His people to enjoy. Yet, Adam and Eve decided to disobey God and this sinful act broke fellowship with God. But God sent His Son, Jesus Christ, to pay for the sin of mankind and all who repent and trust in Him will be forgiven. They will live eternally with Him. This is the great love that made the world for His people.

The existence of God arguments can strengthen your faith as a Christian. Faith is "the assurance of things hoped for and the conviction of things not seen." Faith does not lack evidence but it is unable to grant complete certainty. The arguments for God provide evidence that piles up, pointing to an evidence-based faith. Jesus provided evidence for his disciples as he presented miracles to cure the blind, deaf, and lame. When John the Baptist was in jail, he sent his disciples to ask Jesus if he was the one or if another was to come. John the Baptist was asking Jesus, are you the Messiah? Jesus sent word to John saying, tell John the lame walk, the blind see and the deaf hear. Jesus delivered evidence to show John the Baptist that he was the Messiah. In addition, Jesus presented the evidence of his wounds to the disciple Thomas. He also revealed himself to many people, revealing that He had risen. Having faith does not nullify evidence; instead, evidence reinforces and strengthens our faith. Yes, it is by grace through faith that people are saved and it is an evidence-based faith. Learning the arguments of the scientific evidence works in concert with biblical evidence.

How Does This Answer Apply to My Witness to Others?

Growing in your knowledge of scientific discoveries allows you to engage in meaningful conversations with believers and unbelievers. There is a two-step process in these arguments. The first step is that you can offer good evidence for intelligent design to unbelievers. You are able to engage with people who may not hold the Bible to be reliable, but they attest that science is reliable. These arguments for God allow people to examine the evidence in the natural world. You have the opportunity to ask questions and explain that intelligent design/Christianity provides the best explanation for the things we observe, with the universe having a beginning and fine-tuning to the point that life is permittable.

The second step in the arguments for God opens the door for spiritual conversations. The first step is to reveal there is good reason to believe that there is intelligence that was involved in creating the universe. The second step asks which intelligent designer is the most compelling in creating the universe. It is the transcendent God of the Bible who is free to create by his own self-existent power. An example of someone moving from being an unbeliever to a believer is Allan Sandage. He was one of the most influential astronomers in the 20th century. He served as an assistant to Edwin Hubble and took over the observations of the telescope after Hubble died. He started his scientific career as an agnostic but later became a man of faith. He made clear his belief that science did not prove God but that the evidence they were seeing as scientists fit better with a theistic view rather than a materialistic one. He believed science and religion should work together. Evidence-based faith provides reasons why Christianity better explains the world around us. Jesus provided evidence in miracles and the resurrection. He also provided an understanding of the Scriptures. It was both special and general revelation used in sharing Christianity.

Chapter Review

People often wonder if God exists. In this chapter, you have hopefully learned that the cosmological and fine-tuning arguments support an intelligent design in the universe. That intelligent design is best explained as the God of the Bible because He is an uncaused, immaterial, timeless, and all-powerful God who can create the world out of nothing. By learning these arguments, it provides you with insights to share in meaningful conversations about the God of the Bible. In addition, it can strengthen your walk with God, and it can strengthen your faith. These arguments call you to look at nature to recognize the beautiful world God made for mankind. If a friend is wondering does God exist? You can respond with a confident yes, God does exist. Here is short summation of key points from the chapter:

- The cosmological argument states that things that begin to exist must have a cause. The best explanation of the first cause is the God of the Bible.
- The fine-tuning argument states that the universe is designed to be life-permitting. The designer of fine-tuning is best explained as the God of the Bible.
- The God of the Bible is the best explanation because He is

beginningless, uncaused, timeless, spaceless, changeless, immaterial, powerful Creator of the universe.

- Some people will raise questions and objections to both arguments and attest that God is not the best explanation, but you can refute those answers because Christianity does provide the best explanation.

- These arguments can strengthen your view of God's omnipotence and love and your faith.

- These arguments can help you have meaningful conversations with unbelievers and believers.

Learning Check

Here are five questions to check your learning:

1. Define the cosmological argument.

2. Define the fine-tuning argument.

3. Summarize a scientific discovery that supports an argument for the existence of God.

4. Summarize a biblical insight that supports an argument for the existence of God.

5. Recall a question that promotes meaningful conversations about the existence of God.

Discussion Questions

Here are five questions to prompt a meaningful discussion:

1. How would you respond to a person who says the universe was created by chance?

2. Can something come from nothing?

3. What Scriptures can you use while sharing one of the arguments?

4. What characteristics of God make him the best explanation for creating the universe?

5. How does God's creation testify to His love for you?

Resources for Further Study

- Cosmological Argument videos by William Lane Craig. Available at https://www.reasonablefaith.org/kalam.

- Fine-Tuning Argument videos by William Lane Craig. Aavailable at https://www.reasonablefaith.org/finetuning.

- *On Guard* by William Lane Craig.

- *Why Creationism Still Matters* by Brian G. Chilton.

- *Is God Just a Human Invention? And Seventeen Other Questions Raised by the New Atheists* by Sean McDowell and Jonathan Morrow.

Q3: Is the Bible Reliable?

Tony Williams

> "For we did not follow cleverly devised myths
> when we made known to you the power
> and coming of our Lord Jesus Christ,
> but we were eyewitnesses of his majesty."
> 2 Peter 1:16[19]
>
> "The Holy Scriptures are our letters from home."
> Augustine of Hippo[20]

What We'll Learn

In this chapter, we will examine how we can determine if the Bible is reliable by using techniques that modern reporters, detectives, historians, and attorneys use to decide if historical accounts are reliable. We will also determine what to make of miracles and supernatural events that are contained in the Bible. In our time many claim the book is not what the authors originally wrote, and that it misrepresents, or even makes up history. You likely know by now that simply believing in something doesn't make it true. Like a reporter, a detective, or a historian, we need to examine the evidence for ourselves to see if the Bible is reliable. In this chapter, you will learn:

- How to determine if we have an accurate copy of the Bible.
- How to determine if the events in the Bible are true.
- How to understand miracles and supernatural events in the Bible.

Section One
Answering the Question

Is the Bible We Have an Accurate Copy?

It is assumed that the original writings of the authors of both the Old and New Testaments have been lost to time and that we must rely on copies. Why should we trust the copies we have today? How can we know we have an accurate version of what the authors wrote? Detectives, historians, journalists, and attorneys all recognize the importance of having accurate copies of historical documents. Historical documents like written witness statements, news reports, and legal documents have to be accurate, or people will not know what happened in the past, or how to proceed in the future.

The Old Testament

It is known that ancient scribes who copied the ancient texts were extremely diligent in the way they copied the writings that were passed down to them generation after generation. They had a complex system to ensure they were accurate including counting every word and letter in each scroll and having multiple reviewers verify accuracy. Any errant copies were immediately destroyed.

The oldest complete version of the Old Testament was once believed to be the Leningrad Codex which dated to around 1009 A.D. until, in the 1950's the Dead Sea Scrolls were located by a shepherd in one of the caves near the Dead Sea. Researchers have since located over 40,000 fragments of ancient scrolls in the caves, including copies of every book of the Old Testament except Esther. The writings have been dated to as far back as 300 years before Jesus was born.[21]

Researchers compared the Old Testament writings that were over 2,000 years old to the versions that were only 1,000 years old. They were found to be incredibly accurate. The comparison of the Dead Sea Scrolls has shown to be 95% identical to the Bible that we have now and none of the differences changed the meaning of any of the passages or doctrines. The differences are typically an insignificant grammar shift or a scribal error.[22]

The New Testament

The New Testament can be examined in the same way as the Old. The New Testament first sets forth four "Gospels", Matthew, Mark, Luke, and John. All four provide individual accounts of events from Jesus' birth, life, death, and resurrection so these are extremely important books to examine.

Like the Old Testament, we do not believe we have the original writings of these men, however, we have very good reason to believe the copies we have can be dated to the time when many eyewitnesses of Jesus were alive and could have disputed the contents. All four gospel accounts are now believed to have been written within 20 to 30 years after Jesus' death and resurrection. Because the accounts were so close to the events they describe, and surely circulated to other witnesses, we can conclude the authors likely couldn't get away with lying about what happened. Paul writes in 1 Corinthians 15:6 that Jesus "appeared to more than 500 brothers at one time, most of whom are still alive, though some have fallen asleep."

While some copies contain some scribal errors and grammar changes, we find that the New Testament is also extremely accurate when compared to all of the ancient copies located to date. Dr. Norman Geisler referred to the New Testament as, "simply the best textually supported book from the ancient world."[23] The more ancient copies we have to compare, the more precisely we can verify what the original texts would have looked like and how well they maintained their content over time. If we compare the New Testament writings to other ancient writings, there is simply no comparison.

Christian apologists Josh and Sean McDowell cite a study that provides a helpful illustration of the number of manuscripts we have to compare in the latest version of the classic book, *Evidence that Demands a Verdict*.[24] If we stack copies of other discovered ancient writings like Homer's Iliad or Tacitus's Annals of History, the average stack of ancient writings still in existence would be approximately four feet tall. Compare that to a stack of New Testament writings discovered to date, which would be about one mile high. If we add the Old Testament manuscripts, the height will increase to two and a half miles high![25]

Another impressive fact as we decide how accurate our current Bibles are is the number of ancient writings by persons who quote the gospel passages in letters or other writings. As J. Warner Wallace points out in his book, *Person of Interest*, church leaders in the first 300 years quote over 87% of Matthew, 66% of Mark, 86% of Luke, and 97% of John.[26] This gives impressive evidence that we are reading the same words as the men and women living almost 2,000 years ago who helped build the Church after Jesus ascended into heaven.

Are the Events in the Bible True?

The next question we have to answer if we believe the Bible has been accurately passed down through the generations before us is to determine if what they said is actually true. This question will require methods used by modern detectives, archeologists, and historians to help us decide what to believe. We must examine the evidence left behind to determine if it matches the Biblical account.

Creation

One of the most impressive statements in the Bible occurs in the first sentence of Genesis where the author writes, "In the beginning, God created the heavens and the earth." It is important to understand that for much of human history, mankind has assumed that the universe was eternal, meaning it always existed and always will. This is also a foundational belief in many other religions. Even Albert Einstein believed in an eternal universe that would contradict what Genesis says. However, in the 20th century, scientists have made several observations that show the universe had a defined starting point in time. This so-called "Big Bang" was the beginning of the universe from nothing. Einstein and others had to acknowledge that the universe had a beginning, just as Genesis said it did.

Adam and Eve

If Genesis were true, all human beings would have descended from one man and one woman, Adam and Eve. This might seem like an idea that modern science would quickly dismiss, but thanks to DNA research and the mapping of the human genome, modern science has had to admit that every living human being alive today shares one man and one woman as shared, common ancestors. These have been appropriately called Y Chromosomal Adam and Mitochondrial Eve by scientists investigating human origins. While the time these two common parents lived is still debated the fact that every human alive shares a male and a female ancestor should give skeptics of the Biblical Adam and Eve pause.

The Flood

Aside from creation, the flood story is a major event in world history claimed by the Bible. When Darwin's theory of evolution was made mainstream in the 20th century, the flood account and "catastrophism" geology (understanding that the earth's layers were laid down in a catastrophic flood) lost credibility with many in exchange for uniformitarianism (everything we see in geology is a result of extremely slow processes still occurring today). However, evidence for a global flood is more abundant than you might believe.

Evidence continues to mount that a global flood occurred that led to a rapid depositing of sediments which, under the pressure of the flood water and other layers, became the sedimentary layers we see all over the earth. The fossils we find buried in the sedimentary rocks were buried quickly, in some cases even in the act of eating or giving birth. We find fossils of sea creatures on every continent on earth, and even on mountains as high as the Himalayas.

It is now well documented that people groups from all over the planet have a memory of a catastrophic flood event that included judgment by God or gods and a boat to rescue a small group of people and animals. More than 270 stories from cultures including ancient

Persian, Russian, Chinese, Indian, Native American (North and South America), European, and Pacific Islanders, who were separated from one another by space and time and had the memory before Christian missionaries would have potentially contributed the story to the culture have a memory of the great flood.[27]

People

If the Bible is reliable, there should be evidence for at least some of the people who are so important to the story. According to Biblical archeologist Titus Kennedy, there have been archeological discoveries of about 70 individuals from the Old Testament and 32 individuals from the New Testament.[28] Most of the evidence consists of coins, carved stones, clay tablets, ancient manuscripts, and other artifacts.

Archeology has located evidence for individuals across the now long-gone nations of Old Testament figures Artaxerxes, Darius, and Cyrus (kings of ancient Persia), Balaam (a Moabite prophet), Ben Hadad II and III (kings of ancient Aram), Esarhaddon (king of ancient Assyria), Evil-Murdoch (king of ancient Babylon), Mesha (king of Moab), Osorkon IV (king of Egypt), and Taita/Toi (king of Hamoth). Evidence exists for New Testament figures, including Ananias, Caiaphas, and Annas (high priests of Israel), Herod the Great, Herod Antipas, Herod Agrippa (I and II), Herod Archelaus, and Herod Phillip. There have been other discoveries confirming the existence of James (Jesus' brother and later Bishop of Jerusalem), John the Baptist, Pontius Pilate, Quirinius (governor of Syria), and Tiberius Caesar (emperor of Rome).[29]

Fulfilled Prophecy

Yet another evidence of the accuracy of the Bible exists in the form of fulfilled prophecy. These prophecies predicted the rise and fall of kings and nations and the events of Israel as a nation. One of the most researched types of prophecies relates to Old Testament predictions about the life and death of the Messiah, who we know as Jesus Christ. These prophecies all describe His life including the time and place of His birth, the family line from which He would descend (King David), the power of His ministry, His character, and many of the events of His life and death.

Many books are available on the topic of Biblical prophecy. Some have looked at the odds that one man could fulfill all the predictions. In a book called *Science Speak,* Dr. Peter Stoner calculated the odds of one man fulfilling just 48 of the Old Testament prophecies.[30] Dr. Stoner found that there was a 1 in 10 to the 157th power chance that one man could fulfill all 48 prophecies. 10 to the 157th power means a 1 followed by 157 zeros. While many people could fulfill a few of the prophecies, Jesus can be seen as fulfilling all of them. Many estimates credit Jesus with fulfilling more than 300 prophecies.

Miracles and Other Supernatural Events in the Bible

The Bible describes miracles in both the Old and New Testaments. They are things that go against what we know about the laws of nature. A few examples of the Old Testament would be the creation of the universe, the confusion of tongues at Babel, the Red Sea being divided during the Exodus, and the sun and moon standing still during a battle. Some New Testament examples would be the birth of Jesus to a virgin mother, the healing miracles Jesus performed, Jesus walking on water, and Jesus being raised from the dead.

The Old Testament miracles were often a way for God to display His power and accomplish His will. Jesus also used miracles to demonstrate He was Who He said He was. When Jesus healed the blind, cast out demons, walked on water, and raised people from the dead, the people who saw it were amazed and many believed because of the signs and miracles He performed. These miracles showed that Jesus also had power over nature, sickness, and even death.

How do we deal with these miracles? This is where we can return to the creation story for confidence. As we discussed, the Biblical creation event is the first miracle and certainly the easiest to prove. You live in a created world with laws and laws need a lawgiver. If God can create the universe from nothing, is it a stretch to believe he can divide a sea or walk on water? The first miracle allows all other miracles!

Section Two
Addressing Objections

Tactical Considerations

The objections to Christianity are legion. You have likely heard them from friends, family, or the internet. We should not shrink from these questions. The Bible is full of people who question God and his motivations. There are so many objections, and so many versions of those objections, it would be almost impossible to figure out how to respond to every possible question about the Bible that could be raised.

Secret Service agents have been ensuring that the currency of our country is not counterfeited for generations. The number of ways to make counterfeit money seems to increase every day, and if they had to learn them all they would always be behind the counterfeiters. To improve their ability to identify counterfeit money, the agents focus their learning on real money, so all of the fakes are easy to spot.

The way a Secret Service agent trains can inform how we can deal with objections to the Bible. Know what the Bible says and know the evidence to make a positive case for the reliability and accuracy of the Bible. That way, when someone objects based on the "number of ancient variations" of the Bible, you can respond with the knowledge of just what is meant by those variations (scribal errors, grammar changes) and how none of the variations affect any doctrine in any way.

In his very helpful book, *Tactics*, Christian apologist Greg Koukl provides effective ways to deal with objections.[31] He provides a blueprint for being winsome and encouraging healthy conversations that will get you out of a defensive position and onto a level playing field with the questioner. One of the most effective tactics that he introduces is the idea of simply asking the questioner, "What do you mean by that?" This might sound simple but consider the example below.

A skeptic tells you that there are many different versions of the Bible and asks how you can know if you have the correct version. You can simply respond by asking, "What do you mean by different versions?" This takes the pressure off you and forces the questioner to come up with a definition. Assuming the questioner is just repeating a phrase they heard or read somewhere, it may put them at a loss. You accomplished this without being rude and it gives them a chance to elaborate, if they can.

Koukl provides two more questions for the conversation if needed. The second question is "How did you come to that conclusion?" If the questioner tells you that thousands of ancient copies disagree with one another, you can simply ask them how they came to that conclusion. Again, you are getting yourself off the defensive and forcing the questioner to state their position. Now you are asking them for the evidence. If they respond that they read a book that explained all of this, you can use the third tactic. This includes asking the questioner, "Have you ever considered..." questions. For example, you might ask if they are aware that those variations consist of only minor grammar changes and scribal errors that don't affect any major doctrine. If the person acknowledges that truth, or says they didn't know, you may have gained ground. If they get mad and walk away, you may have "put a stone in their shoe" as Koukl says. The three-question tactic can be altered to almost any objection and can help greatly in your interactions with skeptics.

If you don't know the answer to an objection, at least you have a starting point to investigate. Be courteous and let the other party know that you will research the question and talk again when you know more. There is no shame in this, and they may appreciate the fact that you worked hard to understand the objection, even if you return with an answer that demolishes their position.

Common Objections to the Bible

When it comes to objections to the Bible, I have some good news for Christians. We are not the first generation to ask these questions. And the better news is that generations of truth seekers wrote down how they wrestled with these questions and the answers at which they arrived. Below are some of the more common objections to the Bible and examples of responses inspired by Greg Koukl's *Tactics*. Don't be inclined to memorize them but explore the topics to know the truth and help steer others to it!

Objection: The Bible has changed over time and is no longer accurate. Answer: What do you mean by accurate? If we know the truth about the number of ancient copies, the early dating of the writings, how accurate they are (remember the Dead Sea Scrolls), and how many early church fathers also included copies in writings outside the Bible we know we have a very accurate picture of what was written very close to the time of the events the Bible describes. We have more evidence for the accuracy of the Bible than any other book in ancient history.

Objection: The Bible's version of creation is not accurate based on science. Answer: How did you come to that conclusion? Have you considered the fact that science has uncovered evidence of a beginning in time, space, and matter out of nothing? If all things that begin to exist have a cause, what must the cause of the beginning of all time, space, and matter be? Have you considered it would have to be timeless, spaceless, and immaterial since those things can't create themselves? Whatever created the universe with all of its laws and constants must surely also be super-powerful, super-intelligent, and personal since it chose to create. What does that sound like to you?

Objection: The Bible's version of the arrival and diversity of plants and animals is not accurate based on science. Answer: Have you considered that the evidence in the fossil record supports a cataclysmic flood event with millions of fossils that appear to have been deposited rapidly in a short amount of time? While many scientists are convinced of the evolutionary theory there is a growing number of scientists rejecting the theory due to the evidence discovered in the fossil record and DNA discoveries.

Objection: The Bible is full of contradictions. Answer: What do you mean by contradictions? If the person can come up with an example, it is often the case that they will either misquote the Bible or truly misunderstand the passage. The gospels are often attacked for differences between the two accounts. For example, much has been made of the fact that one gospel reported one angel at the tomb while another reported two. This difference likely comes down to the perspective of the person who is writing or telling the story. This is often a mark of believability for detectives as they consider witness testimony. It shows that the witnesses did not consult one another to make things up but rather, they saw what they saw. Every witness has a unique perspective!

Objection: The Bible writers were biased. Answer: What do you mean by biased? Is it biased for a scientist to write a book about the properties of electrons if they have studied them under microscopic power in a laboratory for years? Do the conclusions the scientist makes about how electrons function become untrue just because the scientist happens to believe them? What did the writers of the New Testament get for the stories they told? For almost all of them, it was torture and death. Not exactly what people tend to be motivated by. Note that there is not one shred of compelling evidence that indicates any of the apostles changed their story to avoid persecution and death.

Section Three
Applying the Answer in Our Walk and in Our Witness

How Does This Answer Apply to My Walk with God?

We set out to investigate the reliability of the Bible. We have truly only scratched the surface of the positive evidence for the Bible's reliability and the evidence against all of the other explanations of reality and natural and human history. As much evidence as there is, some people will never be convinced. The word convinced means that you believe in something or have "faith".

In our time, the term "faith" has had its original meaning altered. Many hear the word and assume it means believing in something despite a lack of evidence. The Bible does not say we should do anything of the kind. The Bible says that "...what can be known of God is plain to them because God has shown it to them. For His invisible attributes, namely, His eternal power and divine nature, have been clearly perceived, ever since the creation of the world, in the things that have been made" (Rom. 1:19-20). So, nature is a witness to God's power.

But God gave us more than just nature, as glorious and awe-inspiring as it is. to provide evidence of Who He is and who we are. He gave us the inspired writings of witnesses throughout history to explain the creation of everything, including man, who fell and brought the world into chaos. He showed up in the Person of Christ Who showed that He had the power over nature, sickness, and even death. The very Creator of the universe willingly allowed His creatures to torture Him and put Him to a grueling death on a cross as a substitute for anyone who would be willing to repent and believe in Him. He allowed normal people to witness this and inspired them to write the story for us so that we would know the way to be reconciled to God.

The Bible makes clear that repentance and faith in Christ is the only way to be reconciled to God. The kind of faith we need if we are to survive the trials of this life is not blind. Hebrews 11:1 says, "faith is the assurance of things hoped for, the conviction of things not seen." Assurance and conviction mean that this faith is confident. We can't confidently walk through this world if we are blind!

John 8:31-32 records Jesus saying, "If you abide in my word, you are truly my disciples, and you will know the truth, and the truth will set you free." 1 Peter 5:8 says, "Be sober-minded; be watchful. Your adversary the devil prowls around like a roaring lion, seeking someone to devour." If you invest your time now to truly investigate the historical and modern evidence for claims of the Bible and learn its content, you can be confident and know the truth for yourself and identify the lies of the enemy who desires your death.

How Does This Answer Apply to My Witness to Others?

If you obtain the kind of faith the Bible prescribes, not blind faith but confident assurance, you will simply have to reflect that light given to you by the Holy Spirit to others. You will find yourself often failing to be intentional enough or share the gospel with enough people, but if you understand what the Bible says about Who God is and what He has done for you it will make it very hard not to be excited and passionate about sharing the good news.

The men I attribute to leading me to faith were teachers, coaches, and a mentor at a job I had. They didn't necessarily walk through the finer points of theology with me but instead provided small doses of facts and experience to support their conclusions. Theirs was a different kind of confidence that made me desire to know what they knew. I eventually got the nerve to ask them. They were loving, and patient, and knew exactly what the Bible said and the evidence to support their position. My life changed trajectory in ways that I may never understand thanks to the light I saw in them that reflected faith in a God they knew died for them on the cross and had the power to save their souls and mine.

If you come to faith in Christ because of the evidence, you will join many who have come before you in an unbroken chain of the faithful for thousands of years who saw and believed and shared the amazing truth with others so they could enjoy reconciliation with God too.

1 Peter 3:15 says, "in your hearts honor Christ the Lord as holy, always being prepared to make a defense to anyone who asks you for a reason for the hope that is in you; yet do it with gentleness and respect." It is right to want to share the gospel with everyone you meet and we are commanded to understand the evidence that exists to support it.

You may someday be an evangelist to people in another country, but you should be a gentle and respectful evangelist to your school, your friends, and maybe even to your family if you open your eyes to this amazing story of a God Who created everything, and Who chose to come in human form to willingly die a horrible death to save those in rebellion from an eternity of pain and sorrow. This is a story everyone needs to know. You can help people know this story is true if you are prepared, and if you share it with a true love for your neighbor and humility under the authority of the Author of life.

Dear student, I encourage you to be a student of God above all things, and the Bible is the best place to find what He has to say about where we came from, what we are designed for, and how to be reconciled to Him. C. S. Lewis once wrote, "I believe in Christianity as I believe that the sun has risen not only because I see it, but because by it I see everything else."[32] I pray you also come to realize that the Bible is reliable and that this fact illuminates your life and the lives of all the people that you meet.

Chapter Review

In this chapter, we learned ways to determine if we have an accurate copy of the Bible, how to determine if the events in the Bible are true, and how to understand miracles and supernatural events in the Bible.

The number of ancient copies, the extremely high degree of accuracy of the copies, and the nearness to the events they describe give us confidence that they are trustworthy versions of the original documents.

The events described by the Bible, including creation, human genetics, the fossil record, evidence for Biblical figures, and especially the evidence for Jesus provide a mountain of positive evidence that the events the Bible described are true.

The fact that the universe (space, time, matter, and energy) has been proven to have a starting point is evidence that the first sentence of the Bible is accurate because we know everything can't come from nothing. We know if a Creator could create the universe from nothing the rest of the miracles listed in the Old and New Testaments are amazing, but certainly not impossible.

Learning Check

Here are five questions to check your learning:

1. What are three things that provide evidence that the Bible has been accurately copied throughout the years?

2. What are three things that provide evidence that the Bible is an accurate account of history?

3. What evidence exists to suggest miracles are possible?

4. What are the three questions from Greg Koukl's *Tactics* to ask skeptics during conversations about the Bible?

5. How does the Bible say we are to defend the reason for our hope?

Discussion Questions

Here are five questions to prompt a meaningful discussion:

1. How would you respond to a person who says the Bible cannot be trusted?

2. Why is knowing the positive evidence for the Bible's accuracy and truth helpful for my walk as a Christian?

3. What steps can I take to be better prepared for challenges to the accuracy and truth of the Bible?

4. What holds me back from being able to share and/or defend the Bible?

5. What questions do I still have about the Bible that I need to investigate for myself?

Resources for Further Study

- *Evidence that Demands a Verdict: Life-Changing Truth for a Skeptical World* by Josh and Shawn McDowell.

- Cold Case Christianity website: coldcasechristianity.com

- Answers in Genesis website: answersingenesis.org

- *Person of Interest: Why Jesus Still Matters in a World that Rejects the Bible* by J. Warner Wallace.

- *Tactics: A Gameplan for Discussing Your Christian Convictions* by Greg Koukl.

Q4: Did Jesus Rise from the Dead?

Brian G. Chilton

> "But the fact is, Christ has been raised from the dead,
> the firstfruits of those who are asleep.
> For since by a man death came,
> by a man also came the resurrection of the dead.
> For as in Adam all die,
> so also in Christ all will be made alive."
> 1 Cor. 15:20–21[33]
>
> "Virtually all critical scholars who address the issue
> indicate how rarely questioned it is that Jesus's disciples
> had some sort of real experiences that made them
> absolutely sure that Jesus had appeared to them after his
> death, enough so to change their lives completely."
> Gary Habermas[34]

What We'll Learn

Since the resurrection holds such weight, can we offer a valid evidential case that the resurrection of Jesus did occur? This brief chapter defends the notion that we can. In this chapter, we will take a very brief journey through the facts that verify the resurrection of Jesus using the acronym RISEN, confront the major objections against the resurrection, before offering a few applications on how the truth of the resurrection impacts our relationship with God and witness to others. You will learn how to build a case for the resurrection of Jesus and have some tools to stand opposed to the skeptical voices of the day. Here are our specific learning objectives:

- You will learn 28 facts concerning the resurrection of Jesus to build a cumulative case for its historicity as a real-life event.

- You will be able to defend the resurrection of Jesus against four of the most common objections given against it.

- You will be able to apply the resurrection to your walk with God and your witness to others.

Section One
Answering the Question

"It sometimes just seems too good to be true," she said with a tinge of reserve as she looked down from her wheelchair. The lady was a wise woman who had accomplished much in her life. However, she had been met with many disappointments. From failed pastors to her failing health, she maintained her faith despite the challenges with which she met over the past five years. She confessed with a tinge of annoyance in her voice, "Many things in life don't live up to expectations. So, why should I believe that this should be the exception?" These were the valid words of a strong, vibrant lady who attended a Bible study group I led at a local skilled nursing facility. "I believe in the resurrection," she continued, "but that doesn't mean that I always understand it, or that it always makes sense in a world of disappointments." All valid points. I can empathize with her sentiments because I have often been a skeptic myself. If you have been taken by some scandalous power grab or simply by someone trying to earn a quick buck, then you can also understand why it is easy to remain skeptical of things that seem "too good to be true." Our world is inundated with telemarketers and identity thieves who chomp at the bit to steal any bit of income from innocent, hardworking people. Therefore, I can completely understand the wise woman's reserve.

The resurrection of Jesus stands as the cornerstone of the Christian faith. It is a gamechanger. This truth is so important that all of Christianity rises and falls upon its validation. The apostle Paul recognized the critical nature of the resurrection of Jesus. He said that if the resurrection was not true, then "our preaching is in vain, your faith is also in vain" (1 Cor. 15:14). He goes on to say that "your faith is worthless" (1 Cor. 15:17) and that your "faith is worthless; you are still in your sins" (1 Cor. 15:17) if the resurrection of Jesus is not true.

Needless to say, the resurrection holds a great deal of weight for Christian belief. Often, scholars debate various interpretations of biblical inerrancy and inspiration. However, at the end of the day, if the resurrection of Jesus did not happen, then those debates are moot. Why? Because Christianity is untrue if the resurrection of Jesus did not happen. However, if the resurrection did happen, Christianity is still true even if the Bible has errors in it.[35]

The Facts (RISEN)

The facts supporting the resurrection of Jesus can be summarized in the acronym, or acrostic, RISEN.[36] RISEN stands for the Records supporting the resurrection, Irritating or embarrassing details that skeptics have difficulty explaining, Sightings of the risen Jesus, Early reports and proclamations about the resurrection of Jesus, and the Newfound faith found in those who encountered the risen Jesus. Each of the five major points will include no less than four data points, with many including much more. Let's dive in.

R = Records

Let's first look at both written and archaeological records that confirm the belief that Jesus resurrected from the dead. This section contains nine data points.

1. Five Independent Testimonies in the Gospels

While we have four Gospels, we have at least five independent sources within them. Scholars label the content that is shared between the Gospel of Matthew and Luke as Q—short for the German word *quelle,* which means "source." This constitutes one source. Then, the content only found in the Gospel of Matthew is a second source. The exclusive content in the Gospel of Mark is the third. The exclusive content in the Gospel of Luke is a fourth. And the Gospel of John makes up a fifth source. When we consider other oral traditions contained within these Gospels that may not be original to the author, then we may have many other lines of testimony. All being said, the more independent testimonies we have pertaining to an event in history, the better attested that event is.

2. Independent Testimonies in the Epistles

Additionally, we have independent sources in the Epistles. Lines of traditions advocated by Paul, Peter, John, and James add additional support to the claim that Jesus had risen from the dead.

3. Extra-Biblical Testimonies in Christian Literature

One thing that shocked me as I was dealing with my own doubts is that so many other people confirmed the resurrection of Jesus outside of the New Testament. Of those who were Christians who support the claim that Jesus had risen from the dead include Clement of Rome, Ignatius,

Irenaeus, Polycarp, and Justin Martyr. Numerous other examples can be given, but those listed wrote within the first few centuries after Jesus's resurrection.

4. Extra-Biblical Testimonies in Non-Christian Literature

Another fact that caused my mind to nearly explode was that non-Christian writers also suggested that something remarkable happened on the first Easter Sunday. Granted, these writers were not believers, so they try to justify it by another means, but that they describe that the early believers reported seeing something is remarkable. Those writers include Tacitus (AD 55–120), Josephus (AD 37–97), Suetonius (AD 69–122), Thallus (AD 52), Pliny the Younger (late first-century AD), and some of the writers of the Jewish Talmud. It's interesting that the Talmud not only indicates that something happened to the body of Jesus, but they also suggest that something bizarre happened with Jesus's birth.[37]

5. The Yehohannon Nail

Archaeologists recently discovered a portion of a young man's heel bone that dated to the first-century. The man's name was Yehohannon. The thing that makes this heel bone so interesting is that the heel bone held the remains of a bent nail and a portion of olive wood that had attached the man to a wooden cross. This find is the first archaeological evidence that supports not only that people were crucified as the New Testament reports, but also that the Romans permitted crucified victims to receive a proper burial. The heel bone buries any claim that the Romans disallowed proper interments of those who had been crucified (pun intended).

6. The Nazareth Decree

The Nazareth Decree is another archaeological find that offers a historical record for the resurrection of Jesus. The Nazareth Decree is a tablet found around the region of Nazareth. The tablet was written around AD 41–54 and contained the decree written by Caesar Claudius. The decree states the following:

> It is my decision [concerning] graves and tombs— whoever has made them for the religious observances of parents, or children, or household members—that these remain disturbed forever. But if anyone legally charges that another person has destroyed, or has in any manner extracted those who have been buried, or has moved with wicked intent those who have been buried to those places, committing a crime against them, or has moved another sepulchre-sealing stones, against such a person, I order that a judicial tribunal be created, just as [is done] concerning the gods in human religious observances, even more so will it be obligatory to treat with honor those who have been entombed. You are absolutely not to allow anyone to move [those who have been entombed]. But if [someone does], I wish that [violator] to suffer capital punishment under the title 'tombbreaker.'[38]

While the decree does not necessarily prove the resurrection beyond a shadow of a doubt, it does show that the belief that Jesus had risen from the dead was early and that it arose in the area where Jesus lived.

7. The Shroud of Turin

The Shroud of Turin (or Shroud for short) is among one of the most compelling, yet controversial, artifacts of all antiquity. The Shroud is a 14-foot-5 inch by 3-foot-7-inch herringbone linen cloth that bears a faint image of a crucified man. The Shroud wrapped a person's body.

Therefore, the front of the body appears on the lower side of the cloth, whereas the back side of the man is inverted on the top side of the cloth.

In 1998, a team of scholars performed a Carbon-14 test of a corner piece of the Shroud. The test showed that the Shroud dated to the medieval ages, far too late to be the Shroud of Jesus. However, modern studies have conclusively shown that the piece of cloth taken for the test did not derive from the original cloth. The piece of cloth tested came from a patchwork to the Shroud that a team of nuns undertook after the Shroud caught on fire. The patchwork effort was well-documented and should have cast the entire test in suspicion from the very outset.

Modern studies have shown that the blood stains on the cloth are genuine Type AB hemoglobin. While Type AB blood is rare in the Middle East at this time, it was very common of ancient Hebrew people. Additionally, tests have confirmed the presence of pollen grains that came from Jerusalem in the first-century. Some of these plants only bloom in March and April in Jerusalem. Additional tests have confirmed that the Shroud dates to the time of Christ, bears similar markings that would have come from Roman flagrums, holds an accurate depiction of the placement of the nails through the hands and feet of the victim, and shows a spear wound—all that matches the biblical depiction of Jesus's crucifixion.

Also, most interestingly, engineers confirmed that the image was produced by UV radiation from inside the body at the level of 34 trillion watts. Not only was there nothing to produce such an image in the medieval or first-century times, but we still do also not have the capacity to produce that level of radiation today![39] While the defense for the resurrection of Jesus does not depend on the Shroud's authenticity, it is of interest to note that recent data seems to strongly suggest that the Shroud housed the body of Jesus of Nazareth. As such—if true—the Shroud not only verifies Jesus's existence, but it also confirms Jesus's crucifixion and the marvelous manner of his resurrection.

8. The Ossuary of James

While note as strong as the other facts, the James Ossuary is still a marvel to behold. Archaeologists discovered the ossuary of James the brother of Jesus.[40] The find is controversial and not without its critics. Nonetheless, if the ossuary proves valid, it adds additional evidence that James the brother of Jesus existed and confirms the burial practices of the Holy Family. That is, they would have placed the body of Jesus in a tomb—just as the NT suggests—and would have prepared the body for its eventual placement in an ossuary.

9. Church of the Holy Sepulchre

In the heart of Jerusalem, one will find a blue-domed cathedral called the Church of the Holy Sepulchre. The church is governed by several factions of the church, including the Eastern Orthodox Church, the Roman Catholic Church, and Armenian Apostolic Church. Within the church, one will find a rotunda named the *Anastasis* (Greek for "resurrection"). Since the days of Helena (AD 248–338), Constantine's mother, it has been believed that the tomb was where Jesus was buried. However, added evidence suggests that Helena was right. It was here that the Romans prior to Constantine placed a statue of Venus to deter the Christians from venerating Jesus at the place. Additionally, recent renovations to the rotunda have shown that the rock upon which the bed was placed belongs to the first-century AD. All being said—even though the Garden Tomb is more peaceful and serene—we know where the empty tomb is located. It is at the Church of the Holy Sepulchre. And guess what? The tomb is still empty!

I = Irritating or Embarrassing Details

Now, let's consider some irritating, or embarrassing details, concerning the resurrection of Jesus. Historians can know whether something is historical according to embarrassing details about the story. This is important because people would not invent something that casts them in a bad light. This section contains five data points.

1. Women Were the First Eyewitnesses

In Jesus's day, women did not enjoy the same freedoms that modern women do. Courts would not listen to a woman's story unless there were two women that testified to the claim. It is astounding to think that the very first witnesses to see Jesus alive were all women (Mark 16:1–8). Of those, the very first was Mary Magdalene (Luke 23:44, 45; John 20:11–28), a woman who seems to have had a past. This is certainly not someone of Jesus's day would invent if it were not true.

2. Joseph of Arimathea Offered Jesus a Proper Burial

In the first-century Middle East, societal customs were built around the community, just as they are today. As such, it was a complete embarrassment if a group or family could not offer a proper burial for their loved one. None of the disciples could offer Jesus a proper burial, except for Joseph of Arimathea. While Joseph of Arimathea was a secret disciple of Jesus, he was a member of the same Sanhedrin that condemned Jesus. As such, it would have been extremely embarrassing for the disciples that it took Joseph of Arimathea to give Jesus an honorable burial (Matt. 27:57–61; John 19:38–42). Furthermore, since Joseph of Arimathea was a public figure, everyone would have known where his tomb was found. There was no shroud of secrecy in this case.

3. The Resurrection Message Started in Jerusalem

The message of the resurrection began early in Jerusalem around AD 33—the year the Jesus was crucified and resurrected. This is important because everyone could check the tomb to see whether it was empty. Furthermore, nearly everyone would have known Jesus and could have spotted him if he was bloodied, mangled, and trying to escape. Additionally, they could have also recognized him if he had indeed risen from the dead. Because the message began in Jerusalem, deceptive practices would not have been as easy to pull off as they would be in other distant locales. This is an irritating detail for skeptics as it is difficult to explain why the disciples would invent a story in a place where it could be so easily debunked.

4. No One Anticipated the Resurrection Before the End of Time

We do not have the space to give this piece of evidence the defense it deserves. Nonetheless, to summarize, studies of messianic expectations have shown that most people expected the Messiah to bring political liberation to their country and to lead them into a new age of perfect peace and Israeli rule. Even though some expected a Messianic priest, no one expected the Messiah to rise from the dead three days after his execution. Some branches of Judaism did anticipate a final resurrection of the dead to accompany the end times. But again—and I cannot emphasize this enough—NO ONE thought that the Messiah would be crucified and rise from the dead on the third day. After the fact, the disciples began to see the clues in the messianic prophecies of the Old Testament, but that came well after Jesus arose from the dead. Why would the disciples conspire to do something that no one expected would happen in the first place? The fact that the Gospels consistently show that the disciples were ignorant to this fact is both embarrassing for the disciples and irritating to skeptics.

5. The Law That a Man Hung on a Tree Was Accursed

Deuteronomy 21:22–23 states that anyone hung upon a tree is accursed by God. Since the early disciples were Jewish believers, why on God's green Earth would they invent a story of their hero as a crucified redeemer? This was the worst possible execution to have for a hopeful messianic leader. Even now, it is ironic that the cross is the symbol of Christianity. The cross—an instrument of torture and death—is a symbol of God's curse. Quite simply, no one can justify the continuance of Christianity without the resurrection. If Jesus had not raised from the dead, no Jewish believer in their right mind would have continued believing that Jesus was the Christ since he would have been condemned according to God's law. However, if Jesus arose from the dead, then he would be vindicated and proven to be God's Anointed. I'll go one step further. If Jesus had not resurrected from the dead, I highly doubt that you or I would have ever even heard the name Jesus of Nazareth.

S = Sightings

The biblical records report a large number of people who encountered the risen Jesus. Let's consider six data points in this section.

1. 500 Eyewitnesses

In the NT creed of 1 Corinthians 15:3–9, a large number of people are reported to have seen Jesus alive at one time. 500 to be exact. If we consider that women were normally not listed among those in public gatherings, then it is conceivable that we could be speaking of 1,000 people or more. If their children were with them, then it is possible that 2,000 people or more saw Jesus alive at one time.

2. Women at the Tomb

As we previously noted, the women at the tomb were the first to see the risen Jesus. So, how many women are we talking about? Most likely, there were at least five women at the tomb. First, there is Mary Magdalene—whom we already discussed (Mark 6:9; Luke 24:10; John 20:18). Second, a woman named Joanna, who was the wife of Chuza (a household manager of King Herod Antipas (Luke 8:3), was at the tomb. She offered financial assistance to the ministry of Jesus (Luke 8:3). Third, unsurprisingly, Mary the mother of Jesus was one of the woman at the tomb. While the Bible does not explicitly state that Mary was there, we can deduce from the fact that since John was a caregiver of Mary (John 19:25–27), that Jesus appeared individually to both Peter (Mark 16:7; 1 Cor. 15:5) and to James (1 Cor. 15:7), that Mary would have been one of the first to see the risen Jesus. She may have been the "other Mary" that the Gospels report. Fourth, Mary the wife of Clopas was at the tomb (John 19:25). Hegesippus as noted by Eusebius argued that Clopas was

Joseph of Nazareth's brother, making Clopas and Mary the aunt and uncle of Jesus.[41]

3. The Disciples

Since Judas Iscariot was out of the picture by this time,[42] Jesus appeared to the remaining Eleven. Additionally, Jesus had appointed 70–72 additional disciples to go out two-by-two (Luke 10:1–24). It is inconceivable that these disciples would not have seen the risen Jesus. They could be part of the 500 mentioned in 1 Corinthians 15. But we cannot know for sure.

4. Sightings Reported by James

In the 1 Corinthians 15 creed, we learn that James saw the risen Jesus. James was not a believer in Jesus's ministry during Jesus's earthly ministry.

5. Family of Jesus

As mentioned previously, we have every reason to believe that Jesus not only appeared to James and his mother, but he must have appeared to his other brothers and sisters—7 altogether (4 brothers and 2 sisters) (Mark 6:3).

6. Sightings Reported by Paul

The 1 Corinthians 15 creed also states that Jesus appeared to Paul, as well. Like James, Paul was initially not a believer in Jesus, but only began to follow Jesus after seeing the risen Jesus.

E = Early Reports

Okay, spoiler alert. We have many more reasons to believe that the report of the resurrection was early—many more than what we can offer in this abbreviated summary. Nonetheless, the believer holds strong reasons to believe that the resurrection message began extremely early in the life of the church. We will offer four data points in this section.

1. NT Creeds

The NT Epistles contain early creedal material that predates the composition of the letters themselves. Even agnostic NT scholar Bart Ehrman concedes that these creeds are early.[43] We have mentioned one of the most important creeds—1 Cor. 15:3–9. But there are numerous other creeds to mention, as well, including Rom. 1:3–4; Rom. 10:9; 1 Cor. 8:6; 1 Cor. 12:3; 2 Cor. 13:13; Phil. 2:6–11; Luke 24:34; Rom. 4:25; Col. 1:15–20; 2 Tim. 2:11–13; 1 Tim. 6:12; 1 Tim. 3:16. And there are many more!

2. Oral Traditions of the Gospels

The Bible developed in a time where paper was sparse. When available, small sheets were available more than entire books in which to write. Because of their circumstances, communities had to largely rely on oral traditions to communicate and pass along the stories and traditions that were important to remember. Often, these traditions would be constructed in a rhythmic pattern, using mnemonic devices to assist in memory. Furthermore, once the tradition was established within the community, each community member was responsible for ensuring that the storyteller accurately passed the story. In my studies, I observed that the "Son of Man" sayings were strongly linked to these oral traditions.

The Son of Man image not only spoke to Jesus's resurrection, but it also spoke to his existence as a heavenly Being, One Who approached and was the representative of the Ancient of Days (Dan. 7:13–14). These oral traditions are every bit as early as the NT creeds, if not earlier.

3. Sermon Summaries in Acts

The sermon summaries of Acts (messages given by Peter and Paul) have been recognized as early oral traditions. They often speak of the resurrection of Jesus and are, therefore, evidence of the early reports of the resurrection.

4. Early Belief That the Tomb Was Empty

As mentioned, the sermon summaries in Acts are early reports pertaining to the resurrection of Jesus. The belief in an empty tomb was among those delivered messages, especially in Acts 13:29.

N = Newfound Faith

The final section discusses the transformation of the disciples after having seen the risen Jesus. Four data entries are found in this section.

1. Transformation of Paul

Paul was not friendly to the Christian faith once it first started. In fact, Paul held the coats of the men who stoned Stephen, one of the first martyrs of the church (Acts 7:58). However, Paul would later become one of the greatest evangelists of the church after seeing the risen Jesus.

2. Transformation of James

Like Paul, James was not a believer in Jesus during Jesus's earthly ministry. However, James would become the first pastor of the Jerusalem Church. What changed him? He saw the risen Jesus!

3. Willingness of the Disciples to Die

Another consideration that must be made is that all the disciples were willing to die for what they had seen. Even when facing the possibility of dying the most painful and exquisite tortures, they did not relent and did not change their stories. They all died for what they knew to be true—that Jesus had indeed risen from the dead.

4. Change of the Day of Worship

Lastly, we must remember that the earliest Christians all belonged to the Jewish faith. It is inconceivable that a good Jew would change the day of worship from the Sabbath day. Yet that is exactly what transpired. The disciples changed their day of worship from Saturday to Sunday morning to commemorate the resurrection of Jesus.

Section Two
Addressing Objections

Thus far, we have observed 28 pieces of evidence that suggest that Jesus of Nazareth literally rose from the dead on the first Easter Sunday. But how well do these proofs hold to the objections weighted against the resurrection. Well, let's see for ourselves by examining four common objections to the resurrection of Jesus.

Objection #1: Did Jesus Really Die on the Cross?

The first objection is one that comes from some Islamic scholars, particularly a Muslim apologist named Ahmed Deedat. Most notably, Deedat made these claims in his 1984 publication titled *Crucifixion or Cruci-fiction?* According to Deedat, Paul implies that "there is nothing that Christianity can offer mankind, other than the blood and gore of Jesus. If Jesus did NOT die, and he was NOT resurrection from the dead, then there can be NO salvation in Christianity!"[44]

But does Deedat's objection hold? Far from it. Crucifixion is by far and away one of the most gruesome ways to die. A person is stripped naked, scourged to the point that their insides are visible,[45] nailed through the wrists and ankles on two wooden beams, and left to die by a combination of blood loss, dehydration, and a shock to the cardiovascular system. According to historical records, no one, except one that was reported by Josephus, survived crucifixion. And even with Josephus's report, of the three people taken down from the cross, only one survived even with immediate medical intervention.[46] Thus, the survival rate for a crucifixion victim is extremely low.

Given the multiple eyewitnesses, the presiding leaders of the Sanhedrin being against Jesus, then the likelihood of Jesus surviving the cross is literally non-existent. Gerd Ludemann deducts that "Jesus' death as a consequence of crucifixion is indisputable."[47] Even John Dominick Crossan, who is a skeptic and leading member of the Jesus Seminar, stated, "There is not the slightest doubt about the fact of Jesus' crucifixion under Pontius Pilate,"[48] and "That [Jesus] was crucified is as sure as anything historical can ever be."[49] Even if there was the slightest possibility that Jesus could have survived the cross, the Roman's spear to his side causing blood and water to flow (a medically accurate portrayal of what would have occurred) would have extinguished any flames of hope that Jesus might have lived (John 19:34). And say that he did survive in the tomb, he would have died immediately as soon as his body was placed. Quite frankly, the idea of Jesus surviving three nights in a darkened tomb with no food or water, no medical attention, and no help is more miraculous than believing God raised him from the dead.

Objection #2: Did Someone Steal the Body of Jesus?

One of the earliest objections of the resurrection was the idea that someone—likely a disciple of Jesus—stole the body of Jesus and made it look like he would resurrect from the dead (Matt. 28:11–15). However, as we noted in our section on the evidences, the disciples did not have a clear understanding of the resurrection at this time. Ironically, the Jewish leaders listened more intently on this point than did the disciples. As noted in the Gospel of John, the disciples' idea of resurrection was cloaked in their eschatology (i.e., end-times beliefs) and not in their expectation for a messianic figure (John 11:24). As such, the idea that someone stole the body of Jesus is absurd. This also does not account for the fact that a large number of people interacted with the risen Jesus, leading to the transformation of former skeptics to men of faith, and empowering the disciples with the confidence to die for what they knew they had seen.

Objection #3: Was the Resurrection a Spiritual Experience?

Some in the more progressive camp of Christianity along with ancient Gnostics claim that the disciples did see something on the first Easter Sunday, but it is contended that they had a spiritual encounter with Jesus rather than a physical one. However, such an objection does not hold weight for several reasons. First, the tomb was found empty, and no body was discovered. Second, the message of the resurrection was first proclaimed in Jerusalem. How would Christianity have survived if the Jewish leaders presented the body of Jesus all the while Christians were proclaiming that Jesus had risen? Christianity would have been dead in the water. Third, when the disciples encountered Jesus, he was able to eat broiled fish (Luke 24:36b) and could be physically touched (John 20:17). Again, this objection flounders quite badly.

Objection #4: Was Jesus's Body Placed in a Shallow Grave?

Finally, John Dominick Crossan argues that Jesus's body was placed in a shallow grave and perhaps eaten by wild animals. Crossan writes, "By Easter Sunday morning, those who cared did not know where he was, and those who knew did not care. Why should even the soldiers themselves remember the death and disposal of a nobody?"[50] While creative, this objection fails on multiple points. First, remember the archaeological artifact of Yehoannon's crucified heelbone? Not only does the heelbone prove that people were crucified, but most importantly, it reveals that the Romans allowed the victim's family to offer them a proper burial. Additionally, Josephus even acknowledged the practice of proper burials. He states, "Nay, they proceeded to that degree of impiety, as to cast away their dead bodies without burial, although the Jews used to take so much care of the burial of men, that they took down those that were condemned and crucified, and buried them before the going down of the sun."[51]

Second, it is absurd to think that as well-loved as Jesus was by his disciples and family, that they would not have considered where Jesus would have been buried. Most assuredly, Joseph of Arimathea—a very public figure—would have told the family and disciples where they could see Jesus's body. Addedly, the Jews placed a Roman guard (a military unit of at least 16 soldiers) to oversee the tomb of Jesus.

Third, the shallow grave theory does not consider the transformation of the disciples that came after seeing the risen Jesus. Therefore, we can say, along with the other objections, that Crossan's shallow grave theory is shallow and needs to be buried. It does not hold to the evidence for the resurrection of Jesus that we have presented.

Section Three
Applying the Answer in Our Walk and in Our Witness

So, what does the resurrection of Jesus mean for us? German theologian Wolfhart Pannenberg is attributed for saying, "The evidence for Jesus's resurrection is so strong that nobody would question it except for two things: First, it is a very unusual event. And second, if you believe it happened, you have to change the way you live."[52] So, how does this impact our relationship with God and others? The resurrection of Jesus finds at least six applications.

First, God exists. Arguing first from the resurrection is an evidentialist manner in proving God's existence, as opposed to the classical version which begins with God's existence. Nonetheless, the resurrection of Jesus is confirmation that God exists and cares about the problems of humanity. The resurrection affirms everything that Jesus said about God since it is the ultimate miracle. Therefore, the resurrection is confirmation that God exists, and that God is all-powerful, all-knowing, and all-loving. We can then rest assured that our relationship with God is real and genuine instead of wishful thinking. Furthermore, we can know that God loves us, and that we can share that love with others.

Second, the resurrection affirms the existence of an afterlife. We could also speak to the thousands of reported near-death experiences found across the globe. However, the resurrection gives us an even deeper glimpse into the afterlife since God defeated the throes of death through Jesus. Having a firm conviction in the resurrection of Jesus thereby alleviates any fears we may have about death. Granted, it does not necessarily remove the anxieties that accompany death, but it can help us cope with our own mortality and the grief we have with those who have passed before us. So, we no longer need to fear death. Rather, we can take comfort in that our relationship with God continues for all eternity because of the blessed hope of the resurrection.

Third, the resurrection gives us hope in that God works and moves within his creation. That is, miracles can and do happen. As the angel told Mary, "For nothing will be impossible with God" (Luke 1:37). No matter what you're facing in life. You can take comfort in knowing that God can work a miracle to meet your needs, even if it means raising a person from the dead.

Fourth, the resurrection of Jesus tells us that our problems are only temporary when compared to the awesome power of our eternal God. Jesus went through the pains of death on Friday. But Sunday was coming. The light of God would shine on the world in a way that no one, save Jesus alone, ever anticipated. Through God, death had died, life one, and love reigned supreme. No matter what problem you're facing today, no matter what mountain you must climb, know that your God is able to do anything, even overcome death itself. Therefore, what do we really need to worry about in life? As Paul states, "If God is for us, who can be against us?" (Rom. 8:31).

The last two applications impact our interactions with others. Fifth, the resurrection verifies the truth of the Christian worldview. Even if the Bible contains minor errors—which I do not believe it does—Christianity is still true because of the resurrection of Jesus. The resurrection is the linchpin upon which the Christian faith stands. Regardless of the thousands of interpretations that are found in the Christian religion, the guarantee of its truthfulness is found in the historicity of the risen Lord. Therefore, we should share the Christian worldview with others because it is based on objective facts. The Christian worldview can withstand any onslaught launched against it. So, you can share your faith with confidence!

Sixth and finally, the resurrection implies that Jesus is the only way to God. No other religious leader can lay claim to defeating death. Only Jesus holds that title. Since Jesus taught various things about God, and since God validated those truths through the resurrection of Jesus, then it stands to reason that Jesus is the only viable pathway to God. Since the resurrection is based on solid facts and this indicates that Jesus is the exclusive pathway to God, shouldn't this behoove us to share our faith with increased passion out of our love for others? If so, what are you waiting for? This information isn't only for your benefit, it's to share with everyone who will listen.

Chapter Review

- In this chapter, you learned 28 facts about the resurrection of Jesus so that you can build a cumulative case to defend its authenticity as a real-life event of history. We used the RISEN acronym (Records, Irritating details, Sightings, Early reports, and

Newfound faith) to defend the resurrection.

- You should be equipped to defend the resurrection against the objections given against it, including the swoon theory, the stolen body theory, the spiritual resurrection theory, and the shallow grave theory. By now, you should be able to see how foolish many of these objections are.

- Finally, you should be able to apply the resurrection to at least six theological and pastoral concepts, relating to God's existence, the authenticity of Christianity, the reality of an afterlife, the miraculous, and the temporal nature of our problems.

Learning Check

Here are five questions to check your learning:

1. What are the letters of the RISEN acronym?

2. List at least three evidences supporting each of the letters in the RISEN acronym.

3. What are the four objections mentioned against the resurrection?

4. What are the responses to the four objections against the resurrection?

5. What are the six applications that the resurrection supports?

Discussion Questions

Here are five questions to prompt a meaningful discussion:

1. Which evidences do you find build the strongest case for the resurrection of Jesus?

2. Suppose you have a family member who holds to one of the objections against the resurrection. How would you respond?

3. What do you make of the statement "Even if the Bible contains minor errors, Christianity is still true because of the resurrection of Jesus"? Do you agree or disagree? Why or why not?

4. What additional applications that the resurrection supports can you think of?

5. Is it possible to share the gospel without the resurrection being true?

Resources for Further Study

- *Layman's Manual on Christian Apologetics* by Brian G. Chilton.

- *On the Resurrection: Evidences* (Volume One) by Gary R. Habermas.

- *The Case for the Resurrection of Jesus* by Gary R. Habermas and Michael L. Licona.

- *The Case for Christ* by Lee Strobel.

- *The Resurrection of the Son of God* by N. T. Wright.

Q5: Is Christianity the Only Way?

Michelle Johnson

"Jesus told (Thomas), 'I am the way, the truth, and the life.
No one comes to the Father except through me."
John 14:6[53]

"In today's open climate, people seem offended by the exclusive
claims that Jesus is the only way to God and the only source of
forgiveness of sin and salvation. This attitude shows that many
people simply don't understand the nature of God."
Josh McDowell and Sean McDowell[54]

What We'll Learn

The Bible quotes Jesus claiming to be "*the* way, *the* truth, and *the* life", and He adds that no one gets to God except through Him (John 14:6). One tiny part of speech, one little, three-letter word (repeated three times) included in this verse, has the power to cause nothing less than a small explosion in discussions today. Jesus claims to be *the* way, not *a* way or *one* way to God but the one and only possible means by which we can get to God. This chapter will answer the question, "Is Christianity the only way?" The discussion will then address common objections to that claim and suggest two arguments that underlie those objections. It will conclude by offering a couple of points of application to a believer's life and their witness. In summary, here are our learning objectives:

1. We will learn three of the common objections to the claim that Christianity is the only way.

2. We will learn what the Bible says about humankind's predicament, God's perfect solution, and what His plan really says about His character.

3. We will learn ways this answer applies to your walk with God and your witness to others.

Section One
Answering the Question

Is Christianity the only way to God? The short answer to that question is "yes." However, that doesn't feel like a helpful or satisfying answer when you are responding to someone who objects to that claim, does it? John records Jesus specifically claiming to be the one and only way to God (He also claims to be the truth and the life!). Jesus and the disciples were gathered to celebrate Passover dinner together. This would also be the night Jesus was arrested before His trial and crucifixion. The disciples were concerned and upset about Jesus going away. Jesus, knowing He was going to return to the Father in Heaven, told them they knew the way. Thomas, one of the twelve disciples, asked how they could know the way. Jesus' answer is recorded in John 14:6: "I am the way, the truth, and the life. No one comes to the Father except through me."

What the Bible Says

In Jesus' answer He chooses to use one very tiny but important word, three times. "The" is a part of speech called an article. The sentence would have been grammatically correct if He had chosen to use "a," but it is important that "the" is used. This communicates the fact that Jesus is the *one* and *only* possible way to God. It is this word that tells us as we read the Bible there are no other possible options. Jesus is making a truth claim, and with that, there is no gray area.

The apostle Peter repeats this claim to a crowd of people in Acts 4:12. The context for this event begins in chapter three. John and Peter were headed to the Temple and a lame man was begging for money. The two men told him they didn't have any money to give him; however, by the power of Jesus's name, they healed the man, and the people around were amazed. This, of course, caught the attention of everyone around, including the religious leaders. They had Peter and John arrested. As Peter explained who Jesus was and how this man was healed, he proclaimed, "There is salvation in no one else, for there is no other name under heaven given to people by which we must be saved" (Acts 4:12). It was wonderful that the lame man was physically healed but Peter made it clear, more importantly, Jesus is the one and only way to God.

Now that we have seen two examples from the Bible that record Jesus' declaration that He is *the* way to God, let's back up a step or two and look at the key question again– "Is Christianity the only way?" One might ask the way to where (or who) or wonder why we even need a way. Here is another way to word the key question: "Is Jesus the only way to God?" The Bible is quite clear in answering the questions of "to who" and "why we need a way at all."

In the Beginning

The book of Genesis is the very first book in the Bible. The first chapter tells of the creation of all that exists. It starts, "In the beginning God created the heavens and the earth" (Gen. 1:1). God has always existed and is the creator of all that is. He created the earth, the stars and moon, the sun, the plants and animals, birds and fish (Gen. 1:2-25). On the sixth day of creation, God created man and woman (Gen. 1:26-28). God is the creator, and men and women are a part of His creation. In just a little while, this fact will be an important point to remember.

All that God created was perfect. Adam and Eve were allowed to live in the beautiful garden God had made. As creator, God gave them the task of working and watching over it on His behalf. He also established guidelines by which they were to live. He told them they we welcome to eat from every plant in the garden except the tree of the knowledge of good and evil. If they ate its fruit, God said the consequences would be death (Gen. 2). Life was exactly as God intended for Adam and Eve, a perfect place to live, a purpose for their energy and time, and a right relationship with Him–the creator of all.

The Bad News

So far, so good. There doesn't appear to be any need for a "way" to God, right? However, we need to keep reading. The third chapter of Genesis continues to document the lives of Adam and Eve. Verse two says Eve was challenged to remember what God had said about eating the fruit from the trees in the garden. The serpent twisted God's words and Eve added words to His command (Gen. 3:1-3). The serpent outright accuses God of lying and convinces Eve that she is missing out by not eating the fruit of the tree of the knowledge of good and evil. Adam and Eve both choose to eat the fruit God had said not to.

By this action, Adam and Eve sinned, and through them, all men and women to follow possess a sinful nature and are sinners. If we jump to the New Testament and the book of Romans, there are two verses that summarize the situation well. Romans 3:23 says everyone has sinned and fails to keep God's perfect moral law. Romans 6:23 reminds us what God had said in Genesis, that the penalty for sin is death. This makes it quite clear why we need a way back to a right relationship with God.

Adam and Eve's relationship with God changed because of their choice. As we continue reading Genesis three, we find them hiding when they hear God coming in the garden (Gen. 3:8-10). After they hide from God, they play the blame game (Adam blames Eve, Eve blames the serpent) when asked what they did (Gen. 3:12-13). God curses the serpent and tells Adam and Eve they will no longer live in the garden, work will now be a struggle, and life events will be difficult (Gen. 3:14-24). Adam and Eve were now separated from the once-perfect relationship they enjoyed with their Creator. Their decision to sin had ruined it.

This answers our questions above: "Why do we need a way?" and "To who do we need a way?" We need a way to God. He is our creator and the one over everything because of that. We need a way because our sin has broken the relationship we had with God.

The Good News

That is a lot of bad news. However, there is really, *really* good news. While declaring the consequences of Adam and Eve's sin, God announces that He has a plan to provide a way for men and women to return to a right relationship with Him. Genesis 3:15 is often interpreted as the first promise of a Messiah–Jesus. The four gospels (Matthew, Mark, Luke, and John) in the New Testament testify to the person, life, ministry, death, and resurrection of Jesus. Jesus, God in the flesh, is God's perfect plan to offer the one and only way back to a right relationship with Himself–the Creator of everything.

Section Two
Addressing Objections

What is one of the worst things you can be accused of in our culture today? Intolerance. No one wants to be accused of being intolerant, exclusionary, or judgmental. But these are three of the loudest objections to the claim that Jesus is the only way to God. Let's talk about each one. After we review these three, we'll discuss a couple of issues that I would suggest are the "real" issues for those who oppose this claim.

Intolerance

First, the accusation that this claim is intolerant. A quick Google search for the meaning of "intolerant" provides a list of similar words. If you are intolerant, you are being disrespectful, bigoted, narrow-minded, uncompromising, and unsympathetic, just to name a few. Each of these adjectives screams of qualities that our culture has rejected and done so very loudly over the last few years. We don't want to be any of these things, nor should we. However, as we will see, the accusation is a false one.

Dennis Hollinger wrote a blog post for the C. S. Lewis Institute that dug behind the accusation of being intolerant.[55] We live in a pluralistic culture. Like no time before, we live everyday with people from all walks of life. Our neighbors might be from India, Kenya, China, or Indonesia. The students who attend your school might follow the teachings of Buddha, Hinduism, or Islam or identify as "none" (non-religious). Hollinger suggests that most of our experiences with our co-workers, neighbors, and fellow students are good. They are people we like; they care about us, they are law-abiding, all, around good members of our community. They just happen to subscribe to a different belief system or follow a different god. Who are we to say that Christianity is the only way to God? We are challenged by Hollinger to decide where our beliefs are rooted. Do we let culture tell us what to think? Emotions or feelings? Or God's word–the Bible? Our pluralistic society demands we be respectful of everyone else and by that they mean we don't disagree or tell them we believe what Jesus' claims. Rebecca McLaughlin addresses the problem of "respect" that our culture demands.[56] She says three things. One, "I think you are wrong" does not have to be either a disrespectful statement or an unkind one. Second, she says we should respect people but not their beliefs if they contradict what God's word says. Third, it is important to remember disagreement does NOT equal disrespect.

Exclusivity

Here's a scenario: you are telling a friend about last week's Bible lesson at youth group. The main verse, John 14:6 had brought clarity that reassured you. Jesus said He is the way, the truth, and the life. There is just one way to God, and you can be sure of it. However, your friend looks weirdly at you and accuses you of being rather exclusive in your beliefs and imposing your preferences on others. What you thought made things clear, your friend sees as a claim that rejects people just because they don't believe as you do based only on something you prefer.

What is the response? We live in a culture that believes we all can have our own 'truth' or live as though what's right for me is right for me and right for you is right for you. This, however, is a self-defeating argument. Tim Barnett, with the Stand to Reason ministry, created a video that addresses this issue. According to Barnett, the problem is wrong thinking. Culture today holds personal preference in high esteem. There is a difference between a preference statement and a truth claim, or, to use Barnett's words, a "reality claim."[57]

Culture treats Christianity's claim as a preference, but it is actually a reality statement. Romans 3:23 says all have sinned. Barnett illustrates his point with ice cream. If you asked me, I would tell you that mint chocolate chip ice cream is the best. You might disagree and tell me strawberry is the best. Those are preference statements. In the case of ice cream, we can each hold our own opinion about which one we prefer. Barnett reminds us Christianity isn't ice cream. It is a truth claim that we are all sinners, and Jesus is the only way to God.[58]

Judgmental

We don't like to be called intolerant or exclusionary. Culture will also object to the claim that Christianity is the only way, saying it is judgmental. This continues to reflect culture's belief that everyone can hold to their own truth. Don't judge me! How often do you hear that? In just a bit we are going to discuss God's character or His attributes and will address this topic more. But, for now, a right understanding that God is the creator, and because He is, He is the one who establishes His perfect moral law and determines the penalty for breaking that law is helpful. God is the rightful and perfect judge.

Intolerance, exclusivity, and judgmentalism are three objections made by our culture in response to the claim that Christianity is the only way. While each response and its history and place in culture is too complicated to explore here, I'd like to suggest there are three, two of which we'll talk about here, issues that lie behind these accusations. The first issue is culture's rejection of absolute truth. We want to define our own truth and our own right and wrong. It makes us bristle when someone else (in this case, God) defines it for us. It might mean that we are living in opposition to that truth. (For more discussion on truth, please see the chapter on truth written by T. J. Gentry.)

Attributes of God

The second issue is really an attack on God's nature or His attributes. When culture objects to the claim that Christianity is the only way, it shows that it really doesn't understand the character of God. This is the issue according to Josh McDowell and his son, Dr. Sean McDowell, who wrote *More Than a Carpenter.*[59] First, let's talk about what an attribute is. When we talk about God's attributes, we mean something that is true of God's very being or nature. McDowell and McDowell suggest when culture objects to Christianity's claim and calls it intolerant or exclusionary, it really asking if a loving God would really send people to hell. Love is most definitely an attribute of God. Our culture relishes the chance to point out God is love to support their chosen cause. Where have you seen this happen? It gets confusing for a Christian, doesn't it? Because, yes, God is love. But it's not a complete picture. God is love; He is also just, perfect, holy, righteous, and more.

A loving God doesn't send people to hell. People choose hell. Remember our look into the pages of Genesis above? In Genesis chapter 3, we saw that Adam and Eve *chose* to sin. They rebelled against the guidelines God had established for them. They ultimately wanted to be their own god and do whatever/however they wanted (sounds familiar, doesn't it?). God still loved them. But, because God is holy, sin and sinners can't be in His presence and because God is just, sin must be punished, and the penalty satisfied. But remember, God is also love, and therefore He provided a plan–through Jesus and his death and resurrection, whereby men and women could have their relationship with Him restored. They need only believe this and accept what Jesus did in their place. Jesus is the only way to God, and what a loving plan that is! But we don't get to pick and choose which attributes we want in God!

Authority

The third 'behind the objection' issue I would like us to consider is a rejection of authority. Do you like being told what to do? Are there others in your life who really know what is better for you, than you yourself? Rejection of authority isn't really a new issue. Listen to any toddler whose parent says hold my hand before you cross the street. What do you often hear? No! How about the teenager whose parent tells them not to hang out with a certain group of friends or be home by midnight. The teenager decides they are better equipped to decide what is best for themselves. Remember Adam and Eve? They decided they knew what was better for them. Eating from the tree of the knowledge of good and evil was something they could handle just fine. Do any of these situations sound familiar?

The truth of the matter is that God created us and everything there is, and because He did, He knows what is best for us. Like Adam and Eve, even we who follow Jesus often feel we know what we can really handle or what would be best. This is wrong thinking that roots itself in a culture that just wants to do whatever it sees fit. But the Bible is quite clear (see the above discussion on Genesis) that God is the creator, and we are a part of His creation. He is, therefore, our authority.

Despite Adam and Eve's rebellion in Genesis 3, God loved them (and all mankind after) so much that He offers a plan that satisfies His justice and holiness and flows from His love, goodness, mercy, and grace and allows men and women to be reconciled to Him. It is His right to establish the *one* and *only* way – and this is through faith and trust in His son Jesus Christ. So, despite our sinful nature's tendency to bristle, we need to submit to the authority of God and agree with His *one* way. The amazing thing about God's plan, or as Rebecca McLaughlin calls it, "the scandal of grace," is that anyone is welcome to come to Him if they come this way.[60]

Section Three
Applying the Answer in Our Walk and in Our Witness

All we've learned is only helpful if we can apply it to our lives and to our witness to others. Here are a few suggestions to apply the truths from above to your life and interactions with those who are lost in today's culture. First, ask yourself if you are willing to submit to the word God? The whole word of God. Are you willing to live your life according to what He says? Do you know what His word says? Begin by praying that God's Spirit will help you understand what His word says. Spending time reading the word of God will reveal to you what God says about living a life that is both pleasing to Him and is best for you. If there are hard or confusing passages, ask your pastor at church or small group leader for help. Biblical illiteracy–the inability to read, understand and apply

God's word, is a huge problem among our churches and Christians today, I challenge you to be a part of the solution. Remember it is God's standard not ours. What He commands is not something we decide or choose based on our preferences. This includes the claim that Christianity is the only way!

Second—this follows closely behind the first one: evaluate how you see God and men and women in relation to each other. In the discussion above, we learned in Genesis that God is the creator of everything. Men and women are part of His creation, as are the plants, animals, and all that exists. We are a very special part of His creation; some even call humans the pinnacle of all He created. It is in God's own image that He created man and woman. A right understanding of God's role as creator and our role as part of creation is key. As the creator, He established His perfect moral law. Breaking this law has a penalty. All of us are sinners (Rom. 3:23). As the creator, He also provides the perfect plan, the one and only way back to Him. It is His right to do so and our choice to accept it, but there is no other way. We need to rightly understand this relationship.

In applying the things we have learned in this chapter; I would like to make a suggestion—remember this is God's word. As believers, we testify to the truth of His word. Often in discussion with unbelievers, those that follow Jesus make what the Bible says their own (intentionally or not). Let me explain what I mean. Take the key question of this chapter. Is Christianity the only way? When answering the questions or discussing the topic the answer should be "Yes, God's word is clear that Jesus is the one and only way" or "Yes, because the Bible says Jesus is the only way and I believe the God's word, I think it is." If you simply answer "Yes, I think Christianity is the only way" others can easily see it as your opinion or preference, which we discussed earlier it is not. It is a truth statement from God's word.

Remind those you talk to about the whole of God's character. When we talked about culture's objection to the claim Christianity is the only way we talked about underlying issues. Culture rejects this claim by attacking the nature of God. They ask why a loving God would send people to hell. By learning the different attributes of God, you will be able to help someone understand God's nature is more that loving, it is perfectly just, righteous, holy, good, merciful and more. God's holiness and perfect justice don't allow for sin in His presence. Adam and Eve chose to sin–and through them, we are all sinners. Because God IS loving, He offers a way for us to be reconciled with Him. Yes, there is only one way–through Jesus, determined (rightfully so) by God. It is our choice to accept it.

Lastly, learn the objections culture will offer when faced with the claim that Christianity is the only way. They will claim it is intolerant, exclusionary, and judgmental. These are hot-button words right now in our world, and no one wants to be accused of being any of these. They have the power to immediately shut down a conversation. Press into some of the underlying issues behind these easy-to-sling accusations and apply the facts about God's rightful authority, His attributes, and the existence of absolute truth to your thinking and response. While culture pushes back and accuses Christianity of being intolerant, exclusionary, and judgmental, the truth of the matter is, according to God's word, we are all sinners but our loving, holy, just, righteous, good God has mercifully provided a way for us to be reconciled to Him.

Chapter Review

This chapter has answered the question, "Is Christianity the only way to God?" The answer is yes, and we looked at why we even need a way back to Him. We have also reviewed three common objections our culture raises in opposition to this claim. In addition to these three objections, we also looked at some of the issues that lie behind these objections. Each objection was addressed, and the issues were explored. God's word has clear and satisfying answers to all of these. The chapter concluded by suggesting points of application to your life and witness to others. Be encouraged; God is who He says He is, His word is true, and He has offered the one and only way back to Him.

Learning Check

Here are five questions to check your learning:

1. What does the Bible say about the number of ways to God?

2. Why does today's culture reject the idea that there is only one way to God?

3. What does the Bible say about mankind's predicament?

4. Why is Jesus the only way to God?

5. Why can't God just accept the "good" things we do and be okay with that?

Discussion Questions

Here are five questions to prompt a meaningful discussion:

1. What is the most significant barrier for you to believe Christianity is the only way to God? What challenges would arise if man got to determine the "standard"?

2. Which attribute of God do you tend to "favor" or "prefer"? Which attribute do you most forget about? How does this affect your thinking about God's plan for salvation?

3. How has culture affected your understanding of what the Bible says?

4. What kind of arguments have you heard against the Bible's claim that Jesus is the only way? How have you responded? How do you wish you had responded?

5. What needs to change in your thinking to align with the Bible's description of God as the creator and mankind as part of creation? What barriers keep you from acknowledging God's authority in your life?

Resources for Further Study

- "Is Christianity the Only Way?" by Tim Barnett. Video available at https://www.str.org/w/is-christianity-the-only-way-.

- "How Can Jesus Be the Only Way?" by Frank Turek. Video available at https://www.youtube.com/watch?v=59nwLXWwhbE.

- Got Questions website: gotquestions.org

- "Is Jesus Really the Only Way to God?" by Dennis Hollinger. Article available at https://www.cslewisinstitute.org/resources/is-jesus-really-the-only-way-to-god/.

- *Confronting Christianity: 12 Hard Questions for the World's Largest Religion* by Rebecca McLaughlin.

Meet the Authors of *Strong Faith*

Michelle Johnson

Michelle Johnson earned a PhD in Theology and Apologetics at Liberty University. She also earned her MA in Theological Studies and her MDiv in Professional Ministries at Liberty University. Michelle graduated from the University of Minnesota with her undergraduate degrees. She and her husband live in Minnesota where they are very active in their local church. In addition to her love of theology and apologetics, Michelle also has a passion for historical studies, particularly the theology of the Patristics. When she is not spending time reading or writing, Michelle can often be found dreaming of her next travel adventure or enjoying a great cup of coffee. Michelle previously served as associate editor and contributor to *Why Creationism Still Matters* (2024).

Brian Chilton

Brian earned a PhD in the Theology and Apologetics and MDiv in Theology from Liberty University, a BS in Religious Studies and Philosophy from Gardner-Webb University, a Certificate in Christian Apologetics from Biola University, and completed Unit 1 of Clinical Pastoral Education at Wake Forest University's School of Medicine. In his spare time, he enjoys reading, working out in his home gym, and watching football. Brian has served in pastoral ministry for over 20 years, works as a clinical hospice chaplain, is an Adjunct Professor of Apologetics at Carolina College of Biblical Studies, and serves as the Editor-in-Chief of Acquisitions for Illative House Press. Brian's previous books include authoring *The Layman's Manual on Christian*

Apologetics (2020) and *Conversations about Heaven* (2023), and serving as general editor and contributor to *Why Creationism Still Matters* (2024).

Tony Williams

Tony has served for over two decades as a police officer in a city in Southern Illinois. He has been studying apologetics in his spare time—also for over two decades—since a crisis of faith led him to the discovery of vast and ever-increasing evidence for his Christian beliefs. Tony received a bachelor's degree in University Studies from Southern Illinois University in 2019. His career in law enforcement has provided valuable insight into the concepts of truth, evidence, confession, testimony, cultural competency, morality, and most of all, the compelling need for Christ in the lives of the lost. Tony plans to pursue postgraduate studies in apologetics in the near future to sharpen his understanding of the various facets of Christian apologetics. Tony previously contributed to *Why Creationism Still Matters* (2024).

Deanna Huff

Deanna is a wife and mother. She is passionate about teaching others to share and defend their faith, drawing on 25 years of experience in the field. She has led many seminars for the Baptist General Convention of Oklahoma, the Oklahoma Ladies Retreat, and the State Evangelism Conference. In addition, she taught high school students for ten years at Christian Heritage Academy, covering subjects such as Bible, Universal History, Apologetics and Philosophy. Deanna earned a PhD in Theology and Apologetics at Liberty University. She holds a Master of Theology in Apologetics and Worldview from Southern Baptist Theological Seminary, a Master of Divinity with Biblical Languages from

Southwestern Baptist Theological Seminary, and a Bachelor of Arts from the University of Oklahoma. Deanna is an active member of Capitol Hill Baptist Church where she co-hosted a podcast called *The Analysis* with Pastor Mark DeMoss. She also co-hosted a podcast with her daughter Ellie Huff called *but why should i care.* She and her husband teach an adult Sunday school class, discipling others in the faith. Deanna previously contributed to *Why Creationism Still Matters* (2024).

T. J. Gentry

T. J. is a pastor, biblical counselor, Christian school teacher and administrator, seminary professor, author, Bible teacher, and Christian book publisher. Married since 1995, he and his wife are blessed with five children and a growing brood of grandchildren. T. J. is a graduate of Southern Illinois University (BA in Political Science), Luther Rice College and Seminary (MA in Apologetics), Holy Apostles College and Seminary (MA in Philosophy), Liberty University (MAR in Church Ministries, MDiv in Chaplaincy, ThM in Theology, PhD in Theology and Apologetics), North-West University (PhD in Theology with Missiology), and Carolina University (DMin in Pastoral Counseling, PhD in Leadership, PhD in Biblical Studies). Serving in Christian ministry since 1984, T. J. is a veteran of the United States Army as a Chaplain Assistant and a Chaplain, and holds board certification as a pastoral counselor. His life verse is Galatians 2:20, "I have been crucified with Christ, and I no longer live but Christ lives in me." T. J.'s previous books include authoring *Thinking of Worship: A Liturgical Miscellany* (2011), *You Shall Be My Witnesses: Reflections on Sharing the Gospel* (2018) *Absent from the Body, Present with the Lord: Biblical, Theological, and Rational Arguments against*

Purgatory (2019), *Pulpit Apologist: The Vital Link between Preaching and Apologetics* (2020), and serving as associate editor and contributor to *Why Creationism Still Matters* (2024).

The Bellator Christi Connection

In addition to our shared faith in Jesus Christ and genuine commitment to helping others know and grow strong in the Christian faith, we (Michelle, Brian, Tony, Deanna, and T. J.) are connected through Bellator Christi Ministries, an online Christian education site founded by Brian that deals with issues in theology, apologetics, philosophy, history, and biblical studies. As your strength coaches (reread the Introduction if you're not sure what that's about), we strongly encourage you to visit bellatorchristi.com and start lifting!

Endnotes

[1] Unless otherwise noted, all quoted Scripture in this chapter comes from either the *New King James Version* (designated as NKJV) or the *Christian Standard Bible* (designated as CSB).

[2] C. S. Lewis, A Grief Observed (London: Faber and Faber, 1961), 20-21.

[3] https://search.yahoo.com/search/real+definition

[4] https://search.yahoo.com/search/reality+definition

[5] https://www.tolkienestate.com/

[6] https://www.dictionary.com/browse/opinion

[7] https://www.blueletterbible.org/lexicon/g225/nkjv/tr/0-1/

[8] Unless otherwise noted, all quoted Scripture in this chapter comes from the *New American Standard Bible*.

[9] Stephen C. Meyer, The Return of the God Hypothesis (New York: HarperCollins, 2021), 25.

[10] C. S. Lewis, *Mere Christianity*, Signature Edition (London: William Collins, 2012), 141.

[11] Allan Sandage, "EDWIN HUBBLE 1889-1953 By Allan Sandage (1989, JRASC Vol. 83, No.6)," 1989, https://apod.nasa.gov/debate/1996/sandage_hubble.html.

[12] Meyer, 115.

[13] Brian G. Chilton, ed., *Why Creationism Still Matters* (West Frankfort: IHP Nexus, 2024), 24.

[14] William Lane Craig, *On Guard* (Colorado Springs: David C. Cook, 2010), 74.

[15] Craig, 100.

[16] Meyer, *Return of the God Hypothesis*, 131.

[17] Eric Metaxas, *Is Atheism Dead?* (Washington: Salem Books, 2021), 44.

[18] Carolyn Weber, *Surprised By Oxford* (Nashville: Thomas Nelson, 2011), 128.

[19] Unless otherwise noted, all quoted Scripture in this chapter comes from the *English Standard Version.*

[20] Augustine, *Exposition of Psalm 91.* The quote reflects a common paraphrase of Augustine's actual words, which are "Letters have reached us too from that city, apart from which we are wandering: those letters are the Scriptures, which exhort us to live well.)

[21] Doug Powell. *Holman QuickSource Guide to Christian Apologetics* (Nashville: Holman Reference, 2006), 191.

[22] Norman Geisler, "Has the Bible Been Accurately Copied Down Through the Centuries?" (August 21, 2017) https://ses.edu/has-the-bible-been-accurately-copied-down-through-the-centuries/#:~:text=(5)%20The%20Dead%20Sea%20Scrolls.

[23] Geisler, 2017.

[24] Josh McDowell and Sean McDowell, *Evidence That Demands a Verdict: Life-Changing Truth for a Skeptical World* (Nashville: Thomas Nelson, 2017).

[25] McDowell and McDowell, 53.

[26] J. Warner Wallace, *Person of Interest* (Grand Rapids: Zondervan, 2021), 103.

[27] Titus Kennedy, "Biblical Figures Found Through Archaeology," (July 13, 2020) https://drivethruhistory.com/biblical-figures-found-through-archaeology/.

[28] Kennedy.

[29] Kennedy.

[30] Peter Stoner and Robert Newman, *Science Speaks* (Chicago: Moody Press, 1976).

[31] Greg Koukl, *Tactics: A Game Plan for Discussing Your Christian Convictions* (Grand Rapids: Zondervan, 2009). All examples and quotes in this section are from pages 19-106.

[32] C. S. Lewis, "They Asked for a Paper," *in Is Theology Poetry?* (London: Geoffrey Bless, 1962), 165.

[33] Unless otherwise noted, all quoted Scripture in this chapter comes from the *New American Standard Bible.*

---

[34] Gary Habermas, On the Resurrection: Evidences, vol. 1 (Brentwood: B&H Academic, 2024), 939. In a footnote on the same page, Habermas also adds the following, "Jesus's central preaching of the kingdom of God, Jesus's crucifixion, and the disciples' experiences afterward are probably the three most clearly established historical facts during this timeframe."

[35] I do not believe that the Bible has any errors in it. As such, I hold to the Chicago Statement of Biblical Inerrancy.

[36] The acronym, or acrostic, used in this material originally appeared in Brian G. Chilton, *Layman's Manual on Christian Apologetics* (Eugene: Resource, 2019), 96–99.

[37] Unfortunately, the rabbis of the Talmud held that Jesus was the product of Mary's discrete relationship with a Roman soldier named Pantera. There is no evidence that this claim is true in any way. The claim was more of a polemic than a historical validation.

[38] Gary Habermas, *The Historical Jesus: Ancient Evidence for the Life of Christ* (Joplin: College Press, 1996), 176.

[39] For more information on the Shroud of Turin, please see Brian G. Chilton, "New Evidence for the Authenticity of the Shroud of Turin" (March 31, 2024) https://bellatorchristi.com/2024/03/31/new-evidence-for-the-authenticity-of-the-shroud-of-turin/.

[40] An ossuary is a family burial box. Had Jesus not raised from the dead, his bones would have been placed alongside those of his family. According to Jewish burial traditions of the first-century, a body was placed in a Shroud and other linens and left in a grave. After a year of decomposition, the family would return and dump the bones into a family ossuary. The family would then inscribe the names of those who were interred in the ossuary (i.e., burial box).

[41] Eusebius, *Hist. Eccl.* 3.11; 3.32.6; 4.22.4.

[42] Judas committed suicide (Matt. 27:3–10).

[43] Bart Ehrman, *Did Jesus Exist? The Historical Argument for Jesus of Nazareth* (New York: HarperOne, 2012), 97, 132, 141, 290–291.

[44] Ahmed Deedat, *Crucifixion or Cruci-fiction?* (n.g., Islamic Propagation Centre International, 1984), ebook.

[45] Many did not survive Roman scourging. Remember, Jewish authorities only flogged a person 39 times. The Romans had no such limitations. Their goal was to break the victim's back.

[46] Josephus, *Life of Flavius Josephus* 75.420–421, in *Works of Josephus,* New Updated Edition, William Whiston, trans. (Peabody: Hendrickson, 1987), 25.

[47] Gerd Ludemann, *The Resurrection of Christ: A Historical Inquiry* (Amherst: Prometheus, 2004), 50.

[48] John Dominick Crossan, *The Historical Jesus: The Life of a Mediterranean Jewish Peasant* (San Francisco: HarperSanFrancisco, 1999), 375

[49] John Dominick Crossan, *Jesus: A Revolutionary Biography* (New York: HarperCollins, 1994), 145.

[50] Crossan, *Jesus: A Revolutionary Biography,* 158.

[51] Josephus, *War of the Jews* 4.317.

[52] Pannenberg's exact quote could not be found. Some believe that the quote may be a summarization of Pannenberg's deductions from his collective works.

[53] Unless otherwise noted, all quoted Scripture in this chapter comes from *Christian Standard Bible.*

[54] Josh McDowell and Sean McDowell, *More Than a Carpenter* (Wheaton: Tyndale, 2009), 151.

[55] Dennis Hollinger, "Is Jesus Really the Only Way to God?" (March 5, 2009) https://www.cslewisinstitute.org/resources/is-jesus-really-the-only-way-to-god/.

[56] Rebecca McLaughlin, *Confronting Christianity: 12 Hard Questions for the World's Largest Religions* (Wheaton: Crossway, 2019), 49-50.

[57] Tim Barnett, "Is Christianity the Only Way?" https://www.str.org/w/is-christianity-the-only-way-.

[58] Barnett.

[59] McDowell and McDowell, 151-152.

[60] McLaughlin, 221.